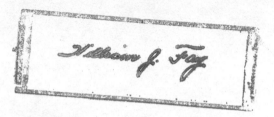

NEW TESTAMENT GUIDES

General Editor
A.T. Lincoln

THE ACTS OF THE APOSTLES

D0813884

THE ACTS OF
THE APOSTLES

I.H. Marshall

Sheffield Academic Press

First published by JSOT Press 1990
Reprinted 1997, 2001, 2003

Copyright © 1990, 1997, 2001, 2003 Sheffield Academic Press
A Continuum imprint

Published by Sheffield Academic Press Ltd
The Tower Building, 11 York Road, London SE1 7NX
15 East 26th Street, Suite 1703, New York NY 10010

www.continuumbooks.com

British Library Cataloguing-in-Publication Data
A catalogue record for this book is available from the British Library

Typeset by Sheffield Academic Press
Printed on acid-free paper in Great Britain by Bookcraft Ltd, Midsomer
Norton, Bath

ISBN 1-85075-372-5

CONTENTS

Preface

This book is based on the Moore College Lectures delivered at Moore Theological College, Sydney, in August 1991. I am grateful to the College for the invitation to give the lectures and for the gracious hospitality which I received during the period of their delivery. With the agreement of the College and of the Anzea Press, the book is being published simultaneously by the Anzea Press in its series of Moore College Lectures and by the Sheffield Academic Press in its series of New Testament Guides.

My understanding of Acts has been greatly helped by having Dr Max Turner as a colleague in Aberdeen during the past five years, and I take this opportunity to express my indebtedness and thanks to him. My thanks also go to Dr Andrew Lincoln for his many helpful comments.

Abbreviations

ANRW	H. Temporini and W. Haase (eds.), *Aufstieg und Niedergang der römischen Welt*
BNTC	Black's New Testament Commentaries
EKKNT	Evangelisch-Katholischer Kommentar zum Neuen Testament
HTKNT	Herders theologischer Kommentar zum Neuen Testament
Int	*Interpretation*
JSNT	*Journal for the Study of the New Testament*
JSNTSup	*Journal for the Study of the New Testament*, Supplement Series
NCB	New Century Bible
NICNT	New International Commentary on the New Testament
NTD	Das Neue Testament Deutsch
NovT	*Novum Testamentum*
TDNT	G. Kittel and G. Friedrich (eds.), *Theological Dictionary of the New Testament*
TNTC	Tyndale New Testament Commentaries
TynBul	*Tyndale Bulletin*
WBC	Word Biblical Commentary

Commentaries and General Works on Acts

COMMENTARIES on Acts from a variety of viewpoints are not lacking! Interpretation of Acts as a broadly historical work with theological significance is found in the work of F.F. Bruce, R.P.C. Hanson, R.N. Longenecker, I.H. Marshall and C.S.C. Williams. The same general approach is found in a number of works written at a more simple and popular level and often providing material relating the teaching of Acts to the present day (G.A. Krodel, W. Neil, J.R.W. Stott, D.J. Williams and W.H. Willimon). An approach which is more sceptical towards the historical value of Acts and places more weight on the creative theological contribution of its author is offered by H. Conzelmann and E. Haenchen. The most recent approach, which examines Acts from the point of view of literary analysis, is found in D. Gooding and R.C. Tannehill.

Commentaries on the English Text
F.F. Bruce, *The Book of the Acts* (NICNT; Grand Rapids: Eerdmans, rev. edn, 1988). The best general purpose commentary.
D. Gooding, *True to the Faith* (London: Hodder & Stoughton, 1990). Gooding attempts a fresh literary analysis of Acts and combines this with a strongly evangelical application.
R.P.C. Hanson, *Acts* (New Clarendon Bible; Oxford: Oxford University Press, 1967). Succinct and useful; one of the first commentators to attempt a balanced assessment of Haenchen's approach.
G.A. Krodel, *Acts* (Augsburg Commentary; Minneapolis: Augsburg, 1986). Non-technical exegesis.
R.N. Longenecker, 'Acts', in F.E. Gaebelein (ed.), *The Expositor's*

Bible Commentary (Grand Rapids: Zondervan, 1981), IX, pp. 207-573. An excellent full-length exegesis in the tradition of Bruce which deserves to be better known.

I.H. Marshall, *Acts* (TNTC; Leicester: Inter-Varsity Press, 1980). Non-technical exegesis.

W. Neil, *Acts* (NCB; London: Marshall, 1973). A basic explanation of the text in simple language.

J.R.W. Stott, *The Message of Acts* (The Bible Speaks Today; Leicester: Inter-Varsity Press, 1990). A unique blend of sound exegesis and modern application.

R.C. Tannehill, *The Narrative Unity of Luke–Acts: A Literary Interpretation*. II. *The Acts of the Apostles* (Philadelphia: Fortress Press, 1990). A very readable literary analysis of how Luke tells his story. Not strictly a commentary.

C.S.C. Williams, *Acts* (BNTC; London: A. & C. Black, 1957). Less thorough than Bruce, but by no means to be overlooked.

D.J. Williams, *Acts* (Good News Commentaries; San Francisco: Harper & Row, 1985). Revised in *New International Biblical Commentary* (Peabody, MA: Hendrickson, 1990). Detailed explanation of the text, simply presented.

W.H. Willimon, *Acts* (Interpretation; Atlanta: John Knox, 1988). Concerned above all with how to preach the disturbing message of Acts today.

Commentaries Requiring a Knowledge of Greek
F.F. Bruce, *The Acts of the Apostles* (Leicester: Apollos, 1991). Revised edition of a work originally published in 1951; strong on textual, linguistic and historical matters, not so full on theology.

H. Conzelmann, *Acts* (Hermeneia; Philadelphia: Fortress Press, 1987). Basic scholarly elucidation of the text, from the same point of view as Haenchen, briefer and not really offering much more to the reader.

E. Haenchen, *Acts* (Oxford: Basil Blackwell, 1971). An immensely detailed, enthusiastically written presentation of the basic question, 'What was Luke trying to do?'

Commentaries in Other Languages that are Important for the Advanced Student
R. Pesch, *Die Apostelgeschichte* (EKKNT; 2 vols.; Zürich: Benziger Verlag; Neukirchen: Neukirchener Verlag, 1986).

J. Roloff, *Die Apostelgeschichte* (NTD; Göttingen: Vandenhoeck & Ruprecht, 1981).

G. Schneider, *Die Apostelgeschichte* (HTKNT; 2 vols.; Freiburg: Herder, 1980, 1982).

A. Weiser, *Die Apostelgeschichte* (Ökumenischer Taschenbuch-Kommentar zum NT; 2 vols.; Gütersloh: Gerd Mohn; Würzburg: Echter Verlag, 1981, 1985).

Other Books Giving an Introduction to Acts or to Luke–Acts
C.K. Barrett, *Luke the Historian in Recent Study* (London: Epworth Press, 1961).

D. Juel, *Luke–Acts* (London: SCM Press, 1984).

I.H. Marshall, *Luke: Historian and Theologian* (Exeter: Paternoster Press, 3rd edn, 1988).

M.A. Powell, *What are they Saying about Acts?* (New York: Paulist Press, 1991).

N. Richardson, *The Panorama of Luke* (London: Epworth Press, 1982).

Collections of Essays Reflecting Recent Scholarship
L.E. Keck and J.L. Martyn (eds.), *Studies in Luke–Acts* (Nashville: Abingdon Press, 1966; repr. Philadelphia: Fortress Press, 1980).

C.H. Talbert (ed.), *Perspectives on Luke–Acts* (Edinburgh: T. & T. Clark, 1978).

C.H. Talbert (ed.), *Luke–Acts: New Perspectives* (New York: Crossroad, 1984).

Works on the Theology of Acts
F. Bovon, *Luke the Theologian: Thirty-Three Years of Research (1950–1983)* (ET Allison Park, PA: Pickwick Publications, 1987).

H.C. Kee, *Good News to the Ends of the Earth: The Theology of Acts* (London: SCM Press, 1990).

J.C. O'Neill, *The Theology of Acts in its Historical Setting* (London: SPCK, 2nd edn, 1970).

Commentaries and other works listed above are not included in the individual bibliographies at the end of each chapter.

1

THE GENRE
AND STRUCTURE
OF ACTS

Introduction

ANYBODY WHO READS or hears the parable of the Good Samaritan for the first time is in for a surprise. The intention of the story, as it was first told by Jesus or first encountered by Luke's readers, was probably to jolt people through sheer surprise into a fresh understanding of how God works and how he wants to see them behave. Even when the story is heard for a second or subsequent time, it still has power to move people by its quality as a story. There is indeed a kind of aesthetic pleasure which is brought about simply by the repetition of what people have already heard, and there is further the fact that some of the finer details may not become clear to them until they hear the story yet again. So too an audience will flock to hear again a musical work which they have heard often enough before. But preachers who take the parable as their theme may find that it has lost its power to shock and influence a congregation who have heard it so often before that they mentally 'switch off' when they begin to hear it. To use the story effectively it may need to be rewritten so as to deal (in a setting of middle-aged respectability) with 'the Good Punk Rocker' or (in an Israeli setting) with 'The Good Member of the PLO', thereby recovering the element of surprise.

But what about reading the Acts of the Apostles? (At this point we may remind ourselves that the same author who recorded the parable of the Good Samaritan also wrote the Acts of the Apostles. I shall follow the normal practice of referring to this person as 'Luke'.) Is Acts meant to function like a parable, so that the first reading is the all-important one? It is certainly true that in the case of Acts Luke was writing, so far as we know, the first work of its kind, and therefore it would be read for the first time as something quite fresh and unusual. Or is it more like a textbook, to be pored over and studied repeatedly? Or has it become so familiar to us that it needs to be rewritten in a different idiom for jaded readers?

Right at the outset we are faced with the question of *how* this book is to be read as a book. It is probably safe to say that anybody who reads this book *about* the book of Acts has already some acquaintance with Acts itself, and therefore comes to it for further understanding of Acts. The assumption is that Acts may need some further light other than that which it sheds upon itself in order to be understood by the reader.

To be sure, the original readers of Acts were not, so far as we know, furnished with a detailed guide to the book that they were about to read. Possibly they needed the ancient equivalent of 'programme notes' such as we get at musical concerts, and perhaps some minimal information about the book was available to them. (We may note in passing that the ancient editors of Greek plays thought it necessary to preface a summary of the plot for the reader.) But what we today require is largely information to help us because we are not the original readers and therefore we need to be put into the same position as them in order to understand the original impact of the book better. So this book is meant to be helpful to people who wonder what is ahead of them as they face Acts for the first time, and to readers who have found problems in what they have already read.

Approaches to the Study of Acts

What are the problems that we need to tackle? Broadly speaking, the study of the book of Acts has moved through three phases.

1. For a long time it was regarded as simply an account of the *history* of the early church, an authoritative history in that it was written by Luke, the colleague of Paul, and in that it was part of the Bible and therefore ultimately inspired by the Spirit of truth. With the rise of modern criticism, this understanding of Acts was called into question; its historical validity could no longer be assumed, but had to be verified, and the result of that process was somewhat negative. So the book of Acts began to be seen more as unreliable history from

which the story of the church could be pieced together only with difficulty. But it was still assumed that the right frame of understanding the book was the historical one. And there was the consequent danger that the book itself was seen merely as an aid to the reconstruction of the historical events that lay at the foundation of the church.

2. Within the last forty years or so, the realization that the Gospels—and with them the book of Acts—are to be seen as primarily *theological* works has become dominant. It was recognized that the Evangelists were men with a message which they couched in the form of an account of the doings of Jesus and his followers, and therefore it made sense to approach their writings in such a way as to lay bare the character of their several theological understandings of Jesus. Acts was included in this approach, and it would be fair to say that the research of the recent past has been largely concerned with the theology of its author. On the assumption that the Gospel of Luke and the book of Acts were written by the same author, it is the theology of Luke–Acts as a whole which has generally been the object of investigation (the only detailed studies of the theology of Acts taken on its own are those by H.C. Kee, *Good News*, and J.C. O'Neill, *Theology of Acts*).

3. Most recently, the study of the Gospels and Acts has taken a fresh direction. There would seem to be fairly general agreement nowadays that the proper place to begin with the study of any book in the Bible is with its character as a *literary* work. That is to say, we encounter Acts first of all as a book that we read, and it is as a piece of literature that it makes its impact upon us. We have to penetrate through it as literature to use it, for example, as a historical source or even as a window on the author's theology. Thus, although study of the first two aspects of Luke–Acts has not ceased, the literary question has come to the fore.

The broad procedure, therefore, will be to commence with the literary questions, to move back to the theological questions, and then to look at the historical problems, before finally raising briefly the question of the significance of the book of Acts for today.

There are, of course, other questions that need to be asked in a full discussion of the book of Acts, but it seems desirable to concentrate on the aspects currently at the focus of scholarly discussion, and to say little about some others which, though important, are less germane or highly technical. I shall, therefore, simply note in passing some topics which will not be developed at length in this Guide, so that more room may be left for the issues which are at the centre of contemporary discussion.

Acts and its Composition

1. *The Greek Text of Acts*

The autographs of all the books of the NT have perished, and we are dependent on a mass of later manuscripts which have been copied from earlier ones with a good deal of sporadic error and deliberate alteration. The science of textual criticism enables scholars to achieve a high degree of probability in reconstructing what the original text must have been. In the case of Acts, however, study of the surviving manuscripts indicates that what we may regard as two somewhat different editions of the book can be traced back to an early period in the transmission, the so-called Alexandrian and Western texts. The former version of the text is that which is normally found in published reconstructions of the text and in English translations, while the latter contains a divergent version of the text—with a fair amount of alternative or extra material sometimes incorporating fresh details in the story (for examples, see the NRSV footnotes at Acts 19.9 and 20.15). Although at various times the Western text has been thought to represent the original wording of Acts or to be one of two versions produced by the original author, the general view is that it represents basically a second-century revision of the original text by an editor who included some additional information (which may or may not be correct) and rewrote the story in minor ways.

2. *The Authorship, Date of Composition and Readership*

Introductions to books of the NT traditionally began with some discussion of the authorship, date and place of composition, and the identity and situation of the readers. These questions are important, and the answers to them do affect the way in which we answer other questions. Unfortunately, certainty about any of them is hard to obtain. It has in fact been notoriously difficult to identify a specific situation for the composition of Acts.

An initial question is the relationship of Acts to the Gospel of Luke. I take the view here that the Gospel and the Acts are two parts of what was originally intended as a single literary work. The alternative possibility is that the Gospel was written first on a stand-alone basis, and only later did the author write a second book which he conceived of as a follow-on to the first. However, various points about the contents of the Gospel indicate that from the beginning it was conceived as the first part of a two-part work.

Opinion is strongly divided on whether the author was, as traditionally believed, the 'Luke' who is mentioned in the NT as a companion or associate of Paul (Col. 4.14; 2 Tim. 4.11), or whether he was some other unknown and unidentifiable person about whom all that we can say is that he had no personal acquaintance with or direct knowledge of Paul. Both opinions are seriously defended in contemporary scholarship. The question is obviously important for assessing the historical reliability of Acts, since authorship by Luke rather than by a later author would obviously favour a positive evaluation of it. However, one of the arguments against authorship by Luke is based on alleged inaccuracies in the portrait of Paul (see Chapter 5 below).

If the authorship is disputed, so too is the date of composition. Dates from the early sixties of the first century (the point at which the story ends with Paul having been held as a prisoner in Rome for two years and not yet having appeared in the Emperor's court) to the nineties are suggested, with the majority of scholars favouring a later rather than an earlier point within this general period.

As for the original readers, some scholars would argue that the actual audience does not matter so much for an understanding of a book as does the *implied* audience, i.e., the audience as envisaged by the author. The general consensus is that Luke was writing for Christian Gentiles in some major city. We shall return to this topic in Chapter 2.

Literary Genre

Leaving aside these questions about the historical circumstances of the composition of Acts, the first question that faces us is the literary one. It has two parts to it: first, the question of the kind of book that Acts is, and secondly, the question of its actual literary structure. We consider first, then, the topic of literary genre.

If a librarian was classifying Acts for insertion on the shelves of the library, where would it be assigned? This question must primarily be answered in terms of the literature of the time when it was written; it would be anachronistic to use a modern type of classification. Thus, if neither the original writer nor his readers understood Acts as a work of fiction, it would be foolish to classify Acts in the fiction section of the library simply because modern scholars argue that the contents are historically inaccurate. It would be perfectly possible for an ancient author to write history inaccurately without intending to write a work of fiction.

The questions of whether Luke was writing what he conceived to be a historically based work and whether he was a reliable writer are in fact frequently confused with one another. J.R.W. Stott (*Message of Acts*, p. 21), for instance, comments in one sentence that Luke 'wrote as a Christian historian', and then, in the immediately following section, which is intended to substantiate and expand on this point, he immediately plunges into the question of whether Luke was a *reliable* historian. But that is not the relevant point in determining whether Luke wrote as a historian. The relevant questions are concerned with the *form* of the work and the author's ostensible *intention*. Whether he had good sources or poor ones, whether he had sound or faulty historical judgment—these are not the questions which settle whether he was acting as a historian.

We have, then, to pose our question about the genre of Acts in the context of the Graeco-Roman world.

1. *Acts as a Historical Novel*
One possible answer to our question is that we should look upon Acts as falling into the category of the *ancient* historical novel or romance.

The resemblances of Acts to ancient novels have long been noted (C.K. Barrett, *Luke the Historian*, pp. 15, 53), but it is only recently that this view has been developed and defended in detail. R. Pervo (*Profit with Delight*) starts from the basis that Acts (and, for that matter, the Gospel also) is full of historical difficulties. He finds great difficulties with the view of E. Haenchen, who, according to Pervo's somewhat exaggerated characterization of his position, held that Luke was a brilliant writer but a stupid historian, and he suggests that the error lies in thinking that Luke was a historian at all. He was not even trying to write history; he was doing something else. What he was doing was to write fiction—doubtless with some contact with reality, as is characteristic of historical novels, but fiction nonetheless. One of his main purposes (but not, of course, his only purpose) was to entertain. Entertainment was the means which he deliberately used in order to write something spiritually and theologically profitable for his readers.

Those who adopt this standpoint point to the features of Acts which are shared with the known literature of this kind in the ancient world—such works were written primarily for entertainment, and therefore they contained the kind of material that would entertain, such as the telling of thrilling episodes—imprisonments and releases, plots and intrigues, mob violence, trials with the cut and thrust of prosecution and defence speeches, dreams and visions, stories of sudden conversions, and so on. Again, there is the journey motif—complete with shipwreck and rescue—which figures in many novels, ancient and modern. There is the use of such literary devices as wit and humour, irony, pathos, oratory. Thanks to the presence of such features as these, Acts is a good story, and it may be simply over-familiarity with the book or our exposure to more sophisticated types of entertaining literature that prevent us from immediately perceiving this point. One motif which is not found at all in Acts is the romantic or erotic aspect. However, it can be observed that this element is not essential to all ancient novels. What is important for Pervo is that in these aspects Acts resembles ancient novels and also resembles the apocryphal, undoubtedly fictional Acts that were written at a later date, such as the *Acts of Paul* or the *Acts of John*.

It is nothing new to recognize that Luke was a good story-teller and that he delighted in telling a good story for its own sake. But this is not the same thing as saying that he set out to write a work of fiction through and through, and in fact there are some basic objections to seeing this as the primary character of Acts (D.E. Aune, *Literary Environment*, pp. 79-80).

One is that Acts must be seen as forming part of a twofold work, Luke–Acts, and we must presume that whatever is true of Acts will also be true of Luke, since there is no indication that the writer adopted a different approach in the two parts of his work.

Opinions differ about whether the preface to the Gospel (Luke 1.1-4) is intended to cover the contents of both the Gospel and Acts (so rightly, in my view, R. Maddox, *The Purpose of Luke-Acts*) or merely those of the Gospel. Even, however, if Luke did not yet envisage the writing of Acts when he composed the preface to the Gospel, the preface to Acts clearly shows that the latter work is

composed as a close sequel to the former, and therefore the presumption is that it is intended to be a work of a similar kind. It is true
that the preface to Acts shows some differences from the kind of
'Introduction to Part II' found in some other ancient works, but these
do not affect the basic point.

But it is patently obvious that Luke was not writing a historical
novel in the Gospel, since he follows fairly closely the sources available to him, and since he makes it clear in the preface that he was
writing a work based on the traditions handed down by eyewitnesses.
Pervo has to deal with this criticism by alleging (a) that the Gospels
are also poor history, and (b) that Luke's claims in the preface are
conventional, and that ancient readers would not have taken them at
face value.

Both of these points fail to convince. On the one hand, the Gospels
have been shown repeatedly to be based on church tradition and to be
churchly documents; their intention is to proclaim Jesus as the Christ
by way of an account of his earthly career. On the other hand, if the
evidence shows that Luke followed sources (like the Gospel of Mark)
with reasonable faithfulness, this would suggest that the claims which
he makes in his preface are to be taken seriously. And with all the
emphasis on truthfulness in the early church and Luke's own stress on
the importance of reliable information, it is highly unlikely that his
claims would have been understood as 'conventional', i.e., not to be
taken seriously.

Secondly, it is difficult to see how Luke could have, so to speak,
'got away' with writing a story about the early church that was not
factually based. The wholesale invention of stories about the early
apostles and evangelists belongs to a later generation which was out of
touch with Christian beginnings.

Thirdly, large areas of Acts simply do not fall into the category of
historical novel writing. They have different concerns. A comparison
of Acts with the apocryphal Acts amply demonstrates the very considerable differences between them. The sheer banality and triviality of
much of the story in the latter is often very conspicuous. In the Acts
of Paul and Thecla, for example, Thecla is placed on a pyre, but a
great thunderstorm puts out the flames; Thecla sees the Lord sitting in
the form of Paul; Paul is thrown to the lions, but one of the lions
turns out to have been baptised by Paul and engages in conversation
with him, and the others are killed or put to flight by a hailstorm.

Fourthly, where Acts does show some of the features found in novels, these are not necessarily features characteristic only of novels, whether individually or as a package.

We can safely regard this view of Acts as not doing justice to its character. What we can say is that this approach rightly brings out the character of Acts as an entertaining and interesting—and even exciting—book to read. Any judgment on it which fails to bring out this feature is to that extent inadequate. This is a book which conveys something of the excitement of the story of the early church. It does not follow that Luke was creating historical fiction in order to entertain, but simply that in telling a story he told it well so that readers would be held by it.

2. *Acts as a History*

A second view of the genre of Acts is that summed up in the phrase 'Luke the historian'. Acts on this view is to be classified with other historical monographs. Here we are, of course, thinking in terms of ancient historical writing rather than modern. One ground for understanding his work in this way is the preface to the Gospel of Luke which is plausibly to be seen as a preface to the whole work. Similar prefaces are found in the work of ancient historians. Against this point L.C. Alexander ('Luke's Preface') has argued that the preface of Luke shows similarities more with the scientific writings of the period than with those of the historians in particular. This would suggest that Luke's book belongs with a kind of middle-brow literature within which the writing of biography was quite possible. Although it is true that the kind of preface found in Luke was paralleled in a much larger area of Greek literature than had previously been brought into the discussion, the fact remains that a person who read, say, the work of Josephus and then turned to Luke would not feel that he or she was moving into a different world. We can perhaps attempt to be too precise about the background to Luke–Acts. Luke could still be writing in the general context of history, and it does not seem to me that the effect of Alexander's work is to exclude this possibility.

Even on a broad view, then, Luke–Acts falls within a set of texts which had a serious purpose, namely, technical or professional prose. This would exclude classifying it as primarily romance or entertainment.

However, at this point we must further observe that the character of

Acts largely resembles that of an ancient historical work. Let us note the features that point in this direction:

a. Whatever its *formal* similarities to other ancient prefaces, the *content* of the preface to the Gospel undoubtedly describes the character of the work as the writing of what Graeco-Roman readers would have regarded as history, based upon some kind of research into, or knowledge of, what had taken place. In other words, although the preface may fall into the general category of 'scientific' prefaces, the subject matter and methods described are historical in nature.

b. The elaborate dating of the 'real' beginning of the story in Lk. 3.1 is reminiscent of a similar phenomenon in Thucydides' *History of the Peloponnesian War*. Other features point to Luke's interest in anchoring his story in the area of world history.

c. The general character of the work lives up to the expectations aroused by the preface. It is a story of a developing historical process.

d. The narrative is punctuated by speeches at significant points.

These points suffice to indicate the general character of the work. As has been rightly observed by M. Parsons ('Acts as an Ancient Novel', p. 409), so far as we know, ancient readers certainly took the book at its *prima facie* value as history rather than as a novel dressed up as history. This of course does not tell us how reliable the work may be in detail. Ancient historians varied enormously in skill and accuracy and would naturally resort to imaginative reconstruction where this was necessary. But clearly there is a real difference between a novel that is only loosely tied to history and a historical work attempting to record what actually happened. We shall look at the question of Luke's relationship to history later; for the moment our concern is purely to identify the literary genre he is using.

3. A Work 'Sui Generis'

We have looked at the two possibilities of whether Acts was intended as entertainment or as a historical work. Neither does justice to the genre of Acts, even though both possibilities contribute to our understanding of the book. We have to come back now to the point that Acts is part of Luke–Acts, and to remind ourselves of the nature of the

Gospel. Unfortunately, attempts to define the genre of the Gospels have not led to any unanimity among scholars.

C.H. Talbert (*Literary Patterns*) argues that the Gospel of Luke falls into the category of a biography, and then claims that Acts follows it as a list or narrative of Jesus' successors and selected other disciples. The effect of this kind of narrative is to show the legitimate understanding of Jesus, the one held by the people here identified as the legitimate successors. Talbert bases this case on a comparison with other ancient literature, specifically the accounts of various philosophers by Diogenes Laertius (c. 250 CE). This view is effectively criticized by Aune (*Literary Environment*, pp. 78-79), who shows that the similarities are very questionable. Nevertheless, Talbert's view does point us in the right direction.

Aune argues a case that the Gospels are best seen as a species of Graeco-Roman biographies, while himself recognizing that they were written with specific aims in view, aims connected with presenting Jesus as the object of the Christian preaching. This means that the historical character of the Gospels is there in the service of a wider purpose.

The same can broadly be said of Acts. Its primary aim is not to entertain nor simply to give a disinterested record of facts; it is concerned with the practical, theological purposes of the early church, and it is an example of good literature being used for a purpose.

Thus we are right to see historical and biographical features in the general form of Luke–Acts, but at the end of the day we have to recognize that the unusual nature of the subject-matter means that the work cannot be simply slotted into any of the existing literary pigeonholes.

To say this is in a sense to move from form to purpose, and to suggest that a characterization of Acts in terms of literary genre may not be the most effective way to get to the bottom of what it is about.

Literary Structure

Recent study of the books of the NT has stressed the importance of grasping them as wholes. In the case of the letters this means endeavouring to understand the flow of the argument so that the 'discourse structure' or 'rhetorical structure' stands out. In the case of a narrative, it means endeavouring to understand the 'narrative flow' of the book, by determining the structure and by looking for ways in which the various parts of the narrative are integrated with one another. In short, the biblical student is asking the literary question of how narratives work, and using insights to determine how the author has intended his narrative to work. What literary techniques have been used? It stands to reason that authors may vary in their capacity to use such techniques, some being more successful than others. There is general agreement that Luke was a careful writer. Some would characterize him as pre-eminently a *littérateur*. Therefore, the search for pattern, design and literary qualities in his work is likely to be a rewarding one. Several different approaches have been taken to this topic.

1. At various times it has been suggested that Luke has followed some kind of *pattern based on the Old Testament* in the composition of the Gospel. Correspondences have been traced, for example, between incidents recorded in Deuteronomy and in the central section of Luke which might indicate that Luke was deliberately following the pattern of incidents there and evoking it for his readers. The theory that a pentateuchal lectionary has provided the pattern for Luke (and for much besides) has also been developed. (For the best statement of this kind of view see M.D. Goulder, *Luke—A New Paradigm*, I, ch. 5.) However, the corresponding suggestion has not been made to the best of my knowledge regarding Acts. We shall not therefore pause to discuss a theory which, even for the Gospel, is dubious.

A different kind of approach in which an OT concept provides the general pattern of thought rather than a strict template is offered by D.P. Moessner. The argument is that Jesus is presented especially in the central chapters of Luke as a prophet like Moses who is rejected by the people. The motif of the journey through the wilderness to the promised land and the symbol of the banquet as a picture of the future consummation are developed. Moessner discusses briefly the application of his theory to Acts (*Lord of the Banquet*, pp. 296-307), suggesting that the careers of Peter, Stephen and Paul can all be seen as those of prophetic figures like Jesus himself. The logic of the work almost demands that there is a reference to the death of Paul and also to the Fall of Jerusalem; indeed the lack of any reference to the latter in Acts is seen as an argument for dating the work before 70 CE.

2. Various systems of *parallelism between different parts of the work have been detected* (C.H. Talbert, *Literary Patterns*). It is

common to see correspondences between the career of Jesus and those of Peter and Paul (and also, therefore, between Peter and Paul) which have the effect of showing that the disciples followed in the footsteps of the Master and that the status of Peter and Paul as witnesses to him is essentially the same. The amount of such correspondence is considerable. However, we should note two things about it.

The first is that this parallelism is not precise in detail. Although the attempt has been made, we cannot draw up tidy systems whereby every incident in one part of the story parallels another in the same order. The subject matter clearly prevented this; Luke was bound by the traditions which he was using.

The second is that a fair amount of the parallelism is due to the simple fact that the careers of the three principal people in Luke–Acts inevitably showed some similarities in that Peter and Paul were engaged in similar work, and the same kind of situations would repeat themselves, and both of them to some extent were consciously imitating Jesus.

Yet, when allowance is made for this, it is still true that Luke appears to have brought out some of these similarities quite deliberately, and therefore we are entitled to claim that one of the things which he was doing was to indicate them—for a number of possible reasons.

3. As a further development of this general type of approach we must note, further, the fact that there are a great many places where the repetition of words and phrases may suggest that Luke is in a way *cross-referencing his material*, so that readers of any one section will be reminded of material elsewhere. Clearly, on an initial reading of the book this type of referencing can only work backwards, but it can also work forwards for readers who come back to the beginning of the book with some memory of what came later from their previous reading. It is here that there can be some difficulty in deciding what does and what does not constitute an allusion. The choice of words may be dictated by any of the following: (a) the limitations of vocabulary, which require that certain words *must* be used for certain concepts and objects; (b) the author's own preference for specific words and expressions, which means that they are repeated simply because they come easily to his mind; and (c) the deliberate use of words to evoke memories of previous parts of the work or to prepare the way for what is to follow. We need to establish some clear

examples of the last of these if we are to prove that Luke uses this method. For example, when only the Lukan Peter (as compared with the Matthaean and Markan) says 'I am ready to go with you *to prison and to death*' (Lk. 22.33), it is hard to resist the impression that this rendering of his words has been formulated with the incidents in Acts 4, 5 and especially 12 in mind.

R.C. Tannehill has produced the most detailed discussion of Luke–Acts from this point of view in a book which is intended to demonstrate *The Narrative Unity of Luke–Acts*. In the first part of this book he tackles the Gospel and traces internal connections in the narrative by means of a study of selected themes in the Gospel. When he comes to treat Acts in his second part, he resorts to commenting on the sections of the text in their written order, drawing out the ways in which they interlock with each other in a variety of ways.

One brief example will illustrate the method. In Acts 11.19-30 Tannehill finds that there is a new development in the story of the church, and that the story 'pulls together threads from the preceding narrative, especially chapters 2 and 8, and weaves them into a tapestry to describe the new phase of the mission' (R.C. Tannehill, *Narrative Unity*, II, p. 146). Key words from 8.4 are repeated to show how the gospel continues to spread. Although the new phase is not due to a mission organized from Jerusalem, nevertheless the Jerusalem church has a secondary relationship with it similar to that in 8.14. Barnabas urges the church to 'stick with the Lord' (cf. 13.43; 14.22; 15.32; etc.), and the church grows, like that in Jerusalem. There is the same stress on teaching (2.42; 11.26); social concern for one another is found in both cases. Barnabas acts as personal link with Jerusalem. The story line of Saul/Paul is also picked up—again Barnabas is involved! The effect of the narrative as a whole is to indicate how a second major centre for mission is developed at Antioch (*Narrative Unity*, II, pp. 146-50). Much of this discussion may not seem very remarkable, and there are times when Tannehill seems to be saying nothing new whatever. However, as the work develops, it does contain some interesting and helpful ideas. For example, Tannehill suggests that the partnership of Silas and Paul represents a unity of purpose between Jerusalem and the mission launched from Antioch (*Narrative Unity*, II, p. 196).

The Story Line

From this survey it emerges that there is vast scope for detecting 'resonances' as we read the story of Acts, with different parts calling others to mind and thus imposing a remarkable unity upon the whole work. None of this, however, has enabled us to define the main story line in the book. Luke has structured his work so skilfully that the commentators have great difficulty in coming to a common mind on how to structure the account or summarize the basic story. But perhaps this is precisely the storyteller's art. A story does not have clear logical divisions like a legal code or a speech in the classical tradition. It flows on, with different themes running severally through it for longer or shorter periods. Nevertheless, it is clear that there are certain turning points in the story.

Of the various attempts to trace a literary structure in Acts, that of D. Gooding deserves mention. He finds the following structure:

1.	1.1–6.7	Christianity and the Restoration of All Things
2.	6.8–9.31	Christianity's Worship and Witness
3.	9.32–12.24	The Christian Theory and Practice of Holiness
4.	12.25–16.5	The Christian Doctrine of Salvation
5.	16.6–19.20	Christianity and the Pagan World
6.	19.21–28.31	Christianity and the Defence and Confirmation of the Gospel

There is a detailed sub-structure in each of these sections. For example, section 3 is divided up into two 'Movements', 9.32–11.8 and 11.19–12.24, and each of these is subdivided into four units. Then some remarkable correspondences and contrasts are traced between corresponding pairs:

1.	Aeneas	9.32-35	Antioch 1	11.19-26
	Peter travels		*Disciples travel*	
	People turn to the Lord		*People turn to the Lord*	
2.	Dorcas	9.36-43	Antioch 2	11.27-30
	Social good works		*Social concern*	
3.	Peter and Cornelius	10.1-48	Herod and Peter	12.1-19
	Religious discrimination		*Religious persecution*	
	Prayer; visions		*Vision; prayer*	
	'Now I realize'	(10.34)	'Now I know'	(12.11)
4.	Peter: The Sequel	11.1-18	Herod: The Sequel	12.20-24
	Criticism	(11.2)	*Quarrels*	(12.20)
	Giving glory to God	(11.18)	*Not giving glory to God*	(12.23)

The correspondences and contrasts here are interesting. They tend to be literary and they impart a kind of unity to the section, but Gooding holds that this unity is more than literary and superficial.

How convincing is this approach? As regards the basic structure of the text, we need to distinguish between the attempts to divide the text into sections and to give descriptive names to them. Quite frankly, if the main headings are meant to represent what Luke was doing in each of these sections, then they simply fail to convince this particular reader. I find it difficult to imagine that, if we asked Luke what he was doing stage by stage in Acts, he would have given us these six sections with these headings describing what he was trying to relate.

As regards the detailed investigation of the narrative, Gooding is doing the kind of thing already practised by Talbert and Tannehill, although it is a weakness of his presentation that he makes no reference whatever to other scholars in his discussion. Gooding draws a parallel between the transfiguration of Jesus half way through the Gospel and the false glorification of Herod half way through Acts and finds this a significant contrast. But he has to say, 'Of course, the similarities and contrasts may not have been intended by Luke. But... there is no reason why we should not compare and contrast them in our own minds' (*True to the Faith*, p. 199). And that puts the problem in a nutshell. How far has Gooding discovered what Luke genuinely intended? Whatever our verdict on all this, the question of Luke's story-structure remains.

My own attempt to summarize the story would be somewhat as follows: Acts begins with the disciples of Jesus and describes how, under the leadership of Peter, they become a Spirit-filled, witnessing and persecuted community in Jerusalem. It moves on to discuss how the movement spreads outside Jerusalem and to non-Jews, partly through persecution, eventually reaching Antioch. Then there begins a series of accounts of missionary work at first based on Antioch. After the first of these accounts there is a pivotal discussion on the requirements to be made of Gentile converts. This is followed by a further account of the spread of the church in the Aegean area. Finally, Paul, the protagonist in the missionary movement, returns to Jerusalem, where he is arrested, and the remainder of the book is concerned with his trials by Jews and Romans, and with his journey to Rome where he intends to appeal to Caesar. Without telling us directly the outcome of that appeal, the book ends.

However, the detailed structure is far from simple, because Luke, being a good storyteller, interlocks the various parts of the story with great skill. The stories of Peter and Paul are carefully intertwined, for example. Or consider how Luke announces the theme of the next section of Acts in 19.21-22 but does not actually finish his account of Paul's activities in Ephesus until 19.41!

This gives the following outline of the story:

1.1–5.42	*Witnesses in Jerusalem*	
1.1–2.47	The beginning of the church	
3.1–5.42	The church and the Jewish authorities	
6.1–11.18	*Witnesses in Judaea and Samaria*	
6.1–9.31	The church begins to expand	
9.32–11.18	The beginning of the Gentile mission	
11.19–28.31	*Witnesses to the Ends of the Earth*	
11.19–14.28	The mission from Antioch to Asia Minor	
15.1–15.35	The discussion concerning the Gentiles in the church	
15.36–18.17	Paul's missionary campaign in Macedonia and Achaia	
18.18–20.38	Paul's missionary campaign in Asia Minor	
21.1–28.31	Paul's arrest and imprisonment	

This outline is based on the threefold pattern in 1.8. It is not a weakness that the third section is disproportionately long, since this is in keeping with where Luke puts the emphasis in his story. The fivefold subdivision in that third section corresponds with the way in which Luke recognizes three distinct missionary campaigns by Paul, the first of which led to the discussion regarding what requirements were to be placed on Gentile converts.

It must be allowed that the points of division could be put elsewhere. For instance, does not 6.1–8.1a, which is played out in Jerusalem, rather belong to the previous section? And should 20.1-38 not be regarded as part of the final section, covering Paul's journey from the missionfield to Jerusalem? Questions like these illustrate the way in which Luke has constructed a narrative that defies precise analysis. Nevertheless, even if the precise points of demarcation are debatable, I would maintain that the basic organisation of the narrative must be very like my proposal, which, incidentally, is somewhat different from that of Gooding.

The structure I have suggested attempts to plot the flow of the narrative. At the same time, there are loose ends in the story that do not appear to be entirely due to the storyteller's art, but leave the reader puzzled in the wrong sort of sense. Why do we not learn what happened to Peter? His career ends in even greater obscurity than Paul's, which is problematic enough. What happened to the Ethiopian convert? There are also other questions that reveal areas of interest where Luke has little or nothing to tell us. For example, what was the nature of the leadership in early Christian churches? What happened in the various churches (other than Antioch) after their initial foundation by the missionaries? Questions like these force us to turn to the problem of why Luke wrote Acts. What was he trying to do? Why did he include some things and exclude others?

Further Reading

L.C. Alexander, 'Luke's Preface in the Context of Greek Preface-Writing', *NovT* 28 (1986), pp. 48-74.

D.E. Aune, *The New Testament in its Literary Environment* (Philadelphia: Fortress Press, 1987).

M.D. Goulder, *Luke—A New Paradigm* (JSNTSup, 20; Sheffield: JSOT Press, 1989).

R. Maddox, *The Purpose of Luke–Acts* (Edinburgh: T. & T. Clark, 1982).

D.P. Moessner, *Lord of the Banquet: The Literary and Theological Significance of the Lukan Travel Narrative* (Minneapolis: Fortress Press, 1989).

M. Parsons, 'The book of Acts as an Ancient Novel', *Int* 43 (1989), pp. 407-10.

R.I. Pervo, *Profit with Delight: The Literary Genre of the Acts of the Apostles* (Philadelphia: Fortress Press, 1987).

C.H. Talbert, *Literary Patterns, Theological Themes and the Genre of Luke–Acts* (Missoula, MT: Scholars Press, 1974).

2

THE SITUATION AND PURPOSE OF ACTS

WHAT WAS THE PURPOSE of Luke in telling this story? Our major source for an answer to the question is the book of Acts itself (together, of course, with the Gospel of Luke); consequently, we enter what is called a hermeneutical circle as we try to find out what the purpose of Acts was from a study of the book and to understand the book of Acts better in the light of what we regard as its purpose.

There may well be several distinct but mutually compatible answers to our question, just as modern authors may write works partly in order to earn some money and partly because they have something that they want to say in print.

Some NT books were written in response to quite specific situations in particular churches; such are the epistles of Paul. Others may be written to a more general audience, just as a modern book may be intended to circulate among a fairly unlimited readership. So far as Luke is concerned, we may ask whether he felt that there was a particular need on the part of his intended readers. Did he write to deal with a specific situation in the church? Was the general character of the work affected by some specific factors? Or was it the case that Luke wrote more because he had something that he wanted to say rather than because he was answering a felt need on the part of his readers?

The History of the Church and its Expansion

To many readers of Acts, it is simply *a history of the early church.* This characterization has a solid foundation in that it recognizes that the contents of Acts are basically intended as historical. Luke is giving an 'account' of what has happened (Lk. 1.1). What is not so defensible is that Luke's aim was *simply* to give a general account of the early church. This view is questionable once we note how limited is the scope of the narrative. There are too many elements of selection and omission to make it likely that Luke was simply recounting a set of facts known to him. It was not a case of somebody asking Luke, 'Tell us how it all began', and Luke simply telling a story in response. The story is a focused one, and we need to discover what are the objects in focus and what has been left out of the viewfinder. As a general history of the early church Acts leaves far too much out.

A much more defensible approach would be to say that Acts is *an account of the missionary expansion of the church* with special reference to the doings of two or three main characters, Peter and Paul being the main protagonists, and Stephen and Philip the minor ones. There is much to be said in favour of this view, especially the fact that a large part of Acts is the story of missionary work over a fairly wide area. But, if this is *the* purpose of Acts, then it fails to account for a large part of the narrative. Specifically chs. 21–28 are concerned with a Paul who is no longer an active missionary but a prisoner experiencing successive trials and eventually being transferred to Rome to appear before the highest earthly court, that of Caesar. Approximately one quarter of the book is devoted to Paul on trial. There is some justification for the view that Luke wanted his readers to remember not Paul the missionary, but Paul the prisoner (R. Maddox, *The Purpose of Luke–Acts*, p. 67). That is probably an exaggeration, but it does direct us to the importance of looking at the purpose of Acts in the light of its conclusion. Successful mission is not the whole story by any means. But we do need to ask why Luke chose to tell the story of the spread of the church.

An Apologia for Paul

Fresh light has been shed on the purpose of the Letter to the Romans by asking questions about the function of its closing chapters that are often neglected by readers. If we adopt the same approach to Acts, namely, to look to its conclusion for some indication of its purpose, we come to the venerable theory that Luke was writing a defence or apologia for Paul.

1. Since the church was being attacked by the Roman authorities and Paul in particular was seen as a dangerous person, it was necessary *to show to them that Christians were law-abiding people and not dangerous revolutionaries.* Acts shows that Paul was not guilty of any crimes against the Roman state. And since the point was so important, it was reiterated in successive trial scenes. Eventually Paul was sent to Rome to appeal to Caesar, although the Roman authorities were not at all sure what crime, if any, he had committed, and suggest that, if he had offended at all, it was against the Jewish laws (Acts 25.24-27).

This motif can undoubtedly be found in the second part of Acts when the Christian missionaries move out into the Roman world (Acts 16.37; 18.14-15; cf. 19.37). It is doubtful, however, that it is more than a minor motif, since Acts contains so much else that is concerned with different interests. Moreover, it is extremely unlikely that the book as a whole was meant to have non-Christian Romans as its principal audience; there is far too much 'in house' material for Christians to make this at all plausible. This view, therefore, finds little, if any, support today as a *principal* explanation of the purpose of Acts. More might be said for the view that part of the purpose of Acts (but only part) was to provide Christians with weapons to use in any clashes with the Roman authorities.

2. P.W. Walaskay (*Political Perspective*) has proposed the contrasting theory that Luke's purpose is *to present the Roman state in a favourable light to Christians* and thus to encourage them to work alongside it. Thus the Roman recognition that there was no real case against Paul is used to commend the Romans and their system of justice to the Christians. But while it is correct that Luke expected Christians to be generally submissive to the human government, there is too much evidence which puts the Romans in a bad light (e.g. Acts 18.17; 24.26), and, when all is said and done, the Roman material forms a small part of Acts (and of the Gospel).

3. There is more mileage in a variant of the previous view. It could be argued that Acts is more concerned with the Jewish charges which were made against Paul. Luke's object was *to show that these Jewish accusations were without foundation.* Paul had done nothing against the ancestral laws of the Jews. The one thing that he admitted was his belief in the resurrection and the messiahship of Jesus (Acts 24.20-21). Even the Roman officials could find no substance in the accusations made by the Jews. In this way, Acts can be seen as an apologia

for Paul against criticisms made from the Jewish side. This view has in its favour the fact that Paul was undoubtedly put on trial by the Jews and that the trial was simply the culmination of a long-standing feud with him. Acts, then, could be intended to help any Christians who were inclined to take these criticisms seriously and also indirectly to furnish an answer to Paul's Jewish critics.

The criticisms of Paul may, of course, have come from another quarter. They could have come from other Christians who were not happy with his understanding of the faith. We know that there was a group of Christians, mainly associated with Jerusalem, who held to a form of Christianity much closer to Judaism in that it had no difficulties about keeping the Jewish law and continuing to live as loyal adherents of Judaism. Acts could be seen as a defence of Paul to his fellow Christians by demonstrating, for example: (a) that he personally kept the law; (b) that he was agreeable to Gentiles keeping sufficient of the law to satisfy the conscientious scruples of law-abiding Jewish Christians; and (c) that his position was endorsed by both Peter and James.

The strength of these views is that they attempt to do justice to the last quarter of Acts (chs. 21–28). But then the question arises as to what the rest of the book is about, especially the eleven chapters or so which are not about Paul at all. For the moment we can say that we have identified one element in the purpose of Acts, although it may require closer definition and although we must look for other purposes alongside it.

4. This view is to be distinguished from that of the Tübingen school in the nineteenth century, according to which Luke was attempting to paint an idealistic picture of the peacable relations between Peter and Paul and thus *to gloss over a breach between Petrine and Pauline factions in the early church.*

The strength of this view is that it recognizes that there was strong tension in the church between two different groups over the admission of the Gentiles, and certainly at one point Peter yielded to pressure and sided with Paul's opponents (Gal. 2.11-14). It can also be claimed with some plausibility that Luke has played down some of the tensions in the church. For example, he has underemphasized the role of the 'Seven' as leaders of the more Hellenistic wing in the Jerusalem church (Acts 6), and he has attributed the separation between Paul and Barnabas to the question of taking John Mark as a missionary colleague

(Acts 15.36-40), when it is often suspected that the quarrel went deeper and involved the question of conditions being laid on Gentile converts (Gal. 2.13).

However, the Tübingen hypothesis is bound up with the untenable postulates of a lasting division in the church between Peter and Paul (contrast how Paul refers to both Peter and Barnabas as colleagues in 1 Cor. 9.5-6; cf. Col. 4.10), and of a late dating of Acts in the second century. The view that even in the first century it was written largely in order to gloss over a quarrel again ignores the fact that the relations between Peter and Paul form a tiny part of Acts.

Encouragement for a Disappointed Church

A very different kind of interpretation of Luke's purpose in Acts is that he was trying to equip the church to deal with a new situation. It is sometimes argued that, whereas the first Christians had expected the *parousia* or heavenly advent of Jesus within a very short period of time and lived their lives within this perspective, the passage of time had led them to doubt the validity of this hope. Were they, then, mistaken (worse still, was Jesus mistaken?), and was the hope of his return an illusion? And what happened to the rest of their beliefs and their lifestyle if this key belief had been falsified by events? Luke can then be seen to have been part of a movement in the early church that was coming to terms with this situation by a reformulation of Christian belief and even by a revision of the story of Christian origins. While not openly abandoning belief in the *parousia*, in effect he marginalized it so that Christian living was no longer dominated by it. Instead he showed that God's purpose right from the start was an orderly progress of events concerned with bringing salvation to the world, and that, although Christians might have to reckon with the absence of Jesus for a long time, this was amply compensated for by the coming of the Holy Spirit. The very fact that Luke wrote a history of the early church in which it was integrated into God's ongoing plan of redemption is part of this process of coming to terms with the delay of the parousia.

It would seem that the original proponent of this view, H. Conzelmann (*The Theology of St Luke*), regarded this attempt to come to terms with the delay of the *parousia* as the guiding motif of Luke–Acts: Luke was consciously trying to carry out this revolution in Christian thinking—as indeed were other Christian theologians who were facing the same problem. Conzelmann argues from the changes that Luke has made in his sources that this was not just a 'development', but rather 'a conscious (*bewusste*) theological attitude to the problem of eschatology' (Conzelmann, *The Theology of St Luke*, p. 86, my amended translation). Luke replaces holding on to the imminent expectation with a proposal of a different kind. It should perhaps be noted that on this view Luke had the very laudable aim of trying to provide the church with an enduring theology that would equip it for the long haul ahead of it in place of a theology which had proved to be mistaken and incapable of carrying the church forward.

An alternative possibility is that this was not, as it were, *the* motive for Luke's composition, but rather a background factor, possibly unconscious or subconscious, which moulded the shape of a work he was writing for different purposes. On this view, Luke was inevitably writing in a certain way because the style of the time demanded it. One may easily cite parallels. For example, I use the thought-forms of the twentieth-century western world rather than any others because this is my intellectual environment.

There are obviously some elements of truth in this hypothesis, with its attempt to do justice to the nature of Luke's work in its context in the second half of the first century. However, it is open to strong criticism if Conzelmann really means that Luke's *conscious* motive (or one of his motives) in writing his work was to offer an answer to the problem caused by the delay of the parousia. It is much more likely that, if a factor at all, it was only *one* of the parameters shaping the character of the work, one of which Luke himself may not have been fully aware. But even in this form the thesis is not acceptable, because it does not adequately account for the shape and character of Luke's theology, which stands much closer to that of his predecessors than this view allows. But Conzelmann's view is too important to be assessed as briefly as this, and we shall return to a more detailed consideration of it later when discussing the theology of Luke (see Chapter 3).

The Writer and his Readers

So far I have done no more than reject some theories about Luke's purpose and pick up some possible subsidiary motives in Luke's work. One weakness in the theories discussed so far is that they do not ask sufficiently deeply about the character, real or implied, of Luke's audience.

The whole of Luke–Acts is addressed to a certain Theophilus, an otherwise unknown person, who is described as having been 'taught' or 'instructed' in the Christian faith. Although this term might refer to the knowledge that an outsider might have of Christianity, it is more likely that it refers to the kind of instruction given to somebody who had joined the church. The whole aim is to give 'certainty' to Theophilus, that is, to confirm what he has already been taught. Can we discover anything about the general character and situation of Theophilus and other readers of Luke–Acts which will help us to understand Luke's purpose?

1. The description of 'Theophilus' as 'most excellent' was a courteous form of address in the higher levels of society. The title may have been used in its narrow sense, as the appropriate form of address to a person holding the rank of a 'knight' in Roman society, or it may have been used as a more general term, but in neither sense would it have been applied to a slave or somebody in the lower strata of society. It is reasonable to assume that Theophilus was typical of at least some of the readers that Luke wished to address.

It is the merit of E.A. Judge (*Social Pattern*) in particular to have insisted that the older picture of the early church as an exclusively lower-class movement, consisting of slaves and other lowly members of society, does not fit the facts. It may be true that 'not many influential, not many of noble birth' (1 Cor. 1.26) belonged to the church, but there was a significant element of such people, and, although they may have been a minority numerically, they were the kind of people who would have had an influence out of all proportion to their numbers. Theophilus, therefore, will have been representative of a wider group of *upper-class influential people* in the church.

2. The general style of the work, with its literary pretensions, suggests that it is written for *an educated part of society* which would appreciate the literary quality. That is to say, although the work could well appeal to readers of different literary levels, there is a deliberate attempt to include a more sophisticated readership.

3. The stress in the Gospel on the relevance of Jesus' teaching to *rich people* is generally taken to indicate that Luke's audience included such. At the same time, it is noteworthy that much of the teaching in the Gospel is addressed to the *poor and lowly*, and it would be fair to

conclude from this that Luke was addressing a fairly mixed group of readers.

4. Luke shows more interest on the whole in *urban society*, although he is recounting the beginnings of a movement which certainly started in a rural setting. The climax of Acts in Rome is not without significance in this respect. The comment that these things did not take place in a corner (Acts 26.26) suggests a Christianity conscious of its important position in the world.

5. Although the traditional view is that Luke was a Gentile, the matter is open to discussion. It can be tackled in two ways. On the one hand, if the author of Acts was the Luke mentioned elsewhere in the NT, we can discuss whether that person was a Jew or a Gentile. However, the most that can be shown from Col. 4.11, 14 is that he could have been a Jew, not that he actually was. On the other hand, we would have to ask whether the evidence of Luke–Acts points to a Jewish or a Gentile author. No compelling argument either way has been produced.

But what about Luke's audience? If he was a Gentile, the probability is that he was writing for Gentile Christians. But in fact, we do not know of any first-century churches which were open to Gentiles but not to Jews. (There may have been Jewish churches which did not welcome Gentiles—or at least admitted them only on certain conditions.) Even when Paul talks about the members of the churches in Macedonia and Achaia as being Gentiles (Rom. 15.27), it is certain that they also included a Jewish element. The discussion of table fellowship supports the view that Luke's audience was *a mixed church of Jewish and Gentile Christians*.

These questions, of a generally sociological kind, are important in assessing what Luke was trying to do and the constraints under which he was writing.

The Legitimation of the Christian Movement

We can now return to the question of the purpose of Acts in the light of its readership and in the light of Luke's own statement (Lk. 1.1-4).

If we turn first to the preface to the Gospel, we find that Luke states there that his purpose was to give certainty to Theophilus regarding what he had already been taught. It is often assumed that this simply means that Luke's purpose was to show that the facts of the matter—

the story of Jesus in particular—were as Theophilus had already received them from earlier sources. In other words, it was the *historical* accuracy of the church's preaching which was at stake. This may well be the case, but it could also be that the general *theological* claims made in the preaching were also being confirmed by Luke through telling a story, based, as he says, on reliable witnesses, which showed that these claims were well founded. For we may be sure that Theophilus was taught not just historical 'facts' but also doctrinal statements and ethical principles. Luke's work is concerned with all of these things. Thus this general view of the purpose of Luke–Acts has the powerful argument in its favour that it corresponds with a reasonable interpretation of Luke's own preface.

Can we take this general approach any further? The 'defensive' type of understanding of Acts has recently come to the fore again in a thoroughly fresh guise. No longer is Acts seen as an attempt to defend a specific individual against attacks. Rather it is seen as *a means of equipping the church as a whole to face threats to its self-confidence.* Acts is concerned with the identity and legitimation of the Christian movement. Undoubtedly, the early Christians, both Jewish and Gentile, were the object of criticism and attack from Jews who did not accept Jesus as the messiah, refused to believe in his resurrection, and disputed that the Christians were truly part of the people of God. Faced by such opponents and by their sheer numbers in comparison with the number of Christians, it is highly likely that some Christians began to doubt their position. Were they really right to believe in Jesus as the messiah when official Judaism rejected him? Could Gentiles become part of the church without being circumcised? Were Jewish Christians not rather apostates? One can well understand early Christians having an identity crisis. Was this why Theophilus needed reassurance, namely because he and other Christians were not sure of the truth of the gospel in the face of attacks from outside?

In this situation a work which retold the story of their origins in order to bring out significant points regarding their true position would be necessary and welcome. It would show, for example: (a) that the coming of the messiah was foretold in the Jewish Scriptures and that Jesus fulfilled the specification; (b) that the resurrection of the messiah was also foretold in Scripture and that it was attested in the case of Jesus by reliable witnesses; (c) that God himself had sanctioned the admission of uncircumcised Gentiles into the church and that any resulting difficulties for scrupulous Jews were removed by the decision of the church that the Gentiles were required not to do things which might offend Jewish susceptibilities; and (d) that Jews who rejected the message concerning the messiah were acting against God in the same way as their ancestors had often done, and therefore their attitude need not be taken too seriously.

This view of the matter obviously has a lot to be said for it. It means that Acts can be seen as having a message both for the church itself and also for Jews who might read it. It has been developed much more thoroughly and systematically by two Australian scholars.

1. R. Maddox argued that Luke's purpose lay in *reassuring his readers about the truth of the gospel*. The attitude of the Jews to them might well make them feel that they were excluded from salvation; after all, if salvation was of the Jews (Jn 4.22), and the Jews as a whole had rejected the possibility that Jesus was the messiah, what grounds had Christians for their counter-claim? To deal with this problem Luke had to show that salvation was being genuinely experienced within the church and that it could be seen as the legitimate fulfilment of God's ancient promises to Israel. This would be an encouragement both to Christian Jews, who felt that they were cut off from their past, and to Christian Gentiles, who were puzzled by the Jewish rejection of Jesus. Luke, then,

> writes to reassure the Christians of his day that their faith in Jesus is no aberration, but the authentic goal towards which God's ancient dealings with Israel were driving. The full stream of God's saving action in history has not passed them by, but has flowed straight into their community-life, in Jesus and the Holy Spirit. If there are apostates and heretics who have cut themselves off from participation in the Kingdom of God, it is not the Christians to whom such terms apply. [Luke writes to show that] it is Jesus, their Lord, in whom the promises of the ancient scriptures are fulfilled; it is Jesus who sends the Holy Spirit, whose powerful influence the Christians actually experience; and it is Jesus alone through whose name salvation occurs (Maddox, *The Purpose of Luke–Acts*, p. 187).

This thesis explains how it is that Luke displays a qualified pro-Jewish orientation side by side with a clear recognition of God's judgment on Judaism for its rejection of the messiah.

Maddox is to be commended for trying to fill out the purpose expressed in Luke's preface: why was it that Theophilus needed the certainty that Luke believed his narrative could give him? The weaknesses in his thesis are the lack of independent evidence that opposition

to the church by Jewish leaders was leading to a crisis of confidence
and the fact that the scope of Luke–Acts as a whole would seem to be
somewhat wider than this single aim.

2. P.F. Esler (*Community and Gospel*) uses what he calls a social-
scientific approach, and his starting point is that social and political
factors, rather than theological ones, were decisive in shaping Luke's
work. He sees the aim of Luke as 'legitimation': Christians 'needed
strong assurance that their decision to convert and to adopt a different
life-style had been the correct one' (*Community and Gospel*, p. 16).
Luke provides this by creating a 'symbolic universe', that is, 'a body
of theoretical tradition which integrates different provinces of
meaning and encompasses the institutional order in a symbolic totality'
(*Community and Gospel*, p. 18). Acts is written for a Christian community, therefore, consisting of Jews and of Gentiles drawn from the
ranks of the 'God-fearers'. Consequently, the important issue is not
that the Gentiles have become the object of mission, but that the
problem of table fellowship between them and the Jews has arisen.
This is the topic that stands at the centre of Esler's discussion. He
argues that Jews absolutely refused table fellowship with non-Jews.
Then he rightly notes how the bone of contention in Acts 10–11 is not
that Peter evangelized Cornelius, but that he ate with him. But for
Esler it is historically inconceivable that Peter did eat with Cornelius.
Therefore, the incident is a Lukan creation to legitimize the existing
practice in the church of his own day which was under pressure as a
result of it. Similarly, the Apostolic Council's acceptance of table
fellowship is unhistorical but very revealing as to Luke's own standpoint. Luke 're-writes the history of early Christianity relating to this
subject and assigns to Peter, James and the church in Jerusalem exactly
the opposite roles to those which they played in fact' (*Community and
Gospel*, p. 107). Two connected issues are the law and the temple.

Here Esler argues that Luke was somewhat inconsistent. He wanted
to argue for Christian fidelity to the law, but had to recognize the
hard facts of history. He was trying to help Christian Jews who were
being criticized for lawlessness by encouraging loyalty to law and
showing that it was in fact the non-Christian Jews who did not keep
the law. With regard to the temple, Luke's problem was eased by the
fact that the temple was no longer there; he could, therefore, take up
the affectionate Jewish memories of the temple, while also recognizing
that non-Jewish Christians had been excluded from the temple and had

developed an anti-temple theology, and while conceding that the future mission of the church depended on the severance of the Christian faith from attachment to the temple.

Two other themes which Esler takes up are the rich and the poor and the question of Rome. He shows that extremes of wealth and poverty were grimly present in the ancient world—and in the church—and that Luke has a paraenetic message here; he is prepared to legitimate the possession of wealth, but at the same time he delivers a powerful call to the rich to care for the poor. Secondly, Esler shows that Luke also writes for the Roman Christians in his church who needed reassurance that being a Christian was not incompatible with allegiance to Rome. We shall come back to these themes in Chapter 4.

For Esler, then, the purpose of Luke lies in reassurance and legitimation, to give assurance to the readers of the validity of their Christian faith vis-à-vis Judaism in particular, and in so doing Luke needs to modify the beliefs (and practices) of his readers and to draw up a theology of the relation of their Christian faith and practice to those of the Jews.

There is much of interest and value in this stimulating presentation. Esler is right to insist that we must look beyond theology to the social situation of the church in order to assess Luke's purpose. There are some questionable details in his thesis; my own view is that he magnifies the historical problems in the story in Acts, and therefore concludes that the problems which he identifies were in Luke's church rather than in the early church as described in Acts. Consequently, he is able to argue that the story in Acts really reflects problems in Luke's church. But suppose that the stories of Peter and Cornelius and of the Apostolic Council are essentially historical; in that case, we can still ask whether Luke has told these stories simply because they happened or because the problems continued. In fact, it seems probable that the Jew–Gentile question with all its ramifications lasted for a long time. There was a hardening of attitudes on the part of Ebionite Christians in Jerusalem, and there was also a tendency for Gentile Christians to become arrogant towards the Jews (cf. Romans), and therefore a continuing need to deal with the problem.

It is apparent that the proposals of Maddox and Esler can sit not too uncomfortably alongside one another, provided that one does not make the mistake of attributing one purpose and one only to Luke. The question remains, what is his primary purpose, if he has one?

Acts as Witness to the Gospel

So far we have ignored any possible clues that we may gain from the opening of Acts. Yet surely the first words of a book are fairly decisive in establishing the character of what is to follow and in putting the reader into the right frame of mind.

Acts begins with a fresh re-telling of the story of the ascension of Jesus. Although the story has different functions in the two books, functioning in its narrative context in the Gospel as an ending which brings it to a closure while serving in Acts as a narrative beginning (M.C. Parsons, *Departure*, p. 194), it undoubtedly forges a clear link between the Gospel and Acts. The reference back to the Gospel, which has recorded 'all that Jesus began to do and teach', suggests that Acts is somehow going to continue the same story. This can be understood in at least two ways.

One possibility is that Acts is a record of *what Jesus went on to do after his ascension*. However, nothing in the story supports this understanding of it. Acts is not about what *Jesus* did, but what his followers did.

Rather, the decisive point is that before his ascension *Jesus gave his instructions to his apostles* (Acts 1.2; it is not certain whether 'through the Holy Spirit' refers to his choice of the apostles or to his instructing of them, but this is not of immediate importance). These instructions are described with care (Acts 1.8). First, the disciples are told to wait in Jerusalem until they are baptised with the Spirit who is also described as a gift promised by the Father. Secondly, they are disabused of the idea that the kingdom is about to be restored to Israel, and they are told (in effect) that when they have received the power of the Spirit they are to be witnesses to Jesus. Thirdly, the scope of their witness is to be worldwide.

It is clear from this that the central instruction is the command to be witnesses. ('You shall be' functions as a command.) The command to wait for the gift of the Spirit is so that they may be prepared for this task. The reference to the places where they are to go indicates the fact that the witness involves mission in the sense that they are not to stay in one place but are to tell people everywhere. Further, the specific reference to Samaria (where the Jewish population was negligible in extent) indicates plainly enough that witness to Gentiles is intended, and the further reference to the ends of the earth should likewise be taken to refer to witness to the Gentiles. The rest of Acts indicates that this is how the words are to be understood.

Witness to Jesus undertaken at the command of Jesus, following the pattern provided by the career of Jesus himself, and empowered by the Spirit, then, is the content. But how is this related to the purpose of Luke? *Why* should he want to make this the theme of the book?

One suggestion is that Luke was basically writing *an evangelistic book*, that is to say, a book that was primarily intended to be put into the hands of non-Christians in order to persuade them of the truth of Christianity (J.C. O'Neill, *Theology of Acts*). There is no disputing that the work can be used in this way. The purposes of confirming a convert in the faith and of leading a person to faith are not that far distant from each other. But this view goes against Luke's own professed aim, and the fact that the book contains a great deal that goes beyond pure evangelism, just as in the case of the Gospel, suggests that Luke was concerned to tell more of the story of Jesus and the church's witness to him rather than simply those elements which were important evangelistically.

Another possibility is that all this is part of the original purpose outlined in the prologue to Luke. There Theophilus was to be given an orderly account of the things that had been happening so that he might know that what he had heard previously was true. So he is first given an account of the life of Jesus told in such a way as *to confirm the truth of the gospel*, and then an account of how witness was borne to him in a way which further confirms its truth.

Here, therefore, we link up with the significant thesis of W.C. van Unnik, which sees 'The "book of Acts" [as] the Confirmation of the Gospel'. For van Unnik, the stress lies on the way in which Acts shows how the gap between Jesus and a later generation in a wider geographical area is bridged, with the key words being 'salvation' and 'witness'. This thesis is of considerable merit in offering a unified view of the purpose of Acts, but it does not go all the way. It places the accent on salvation and the experience of it. The question is rather whether the accent should not lie equally if not more on witness.

We can then say that Luke presented Acts in the form of the story of how the church received and obeyed the command to bear witness to Jesus. But, having identified *what* Luke was doing, we still face the question as to *why* he did it. What was his purpose in so doing?

It would seem that a number of purposes come together in Luke's presentation of the witness to Jesus in Acts. We may sum them up as follows:

1. The central purpose of Luke–Acts is to give the original readers confidence that *the Christian message* which they have heard and accepted *is valid and true*—both as a record of what has happened and in its theological significance as the gospel of divine salvation. To this end Luke had to tell both the story of Jesus and the story of the witness of the church which actually brought salvation to those who heard it. Acts thus falls into the category of instruction, based on a historical record and with a strongly persuasive intent. Its primary function is to help people who are already believers. But whereas other Evangelists thought it sufficient to write a Gospel dealing with the mission of Jesus, Luke saw that it was necessary to show how his mission needed to be complemented by the witness of the church; the witness of the church, proclaiming and teaching about Jesus, is indispensable to a full knowledge of him.

2. As part of this broad purpose it is clear that Luke–Acts could have a secondary *evangelistic* function for people who were not yet believers. The line between confirming the nascent faith of believers and commending the gospel to those who do not yet believe is manifestly a thin one. The commendation that Luke gives to devout Judaism may indicate that the work was intended to appeal to Jews and proselytes, but equally the work contains material that speaks evangelistically to non-Jews.

3. Within this basic theme of confirmation of the gospel, a particular theme in Acts is to show that the church, composed of Jews and Gentiles, *stands in continuity with the saving plan of God*, as revealed in the Jewish Scriptures, that the church is the legitimate fulfilment of the hopes of Israel, and that the principle that Gentiles do not need to be circumcised is divinely willed and should cause no problems for Jewish believers. Jesus is the messiah and the church is the people of God, despite the failure of Judaism generally to believe in him. This aspect of Acts is partly meant to equip the church to deal with Jewish criticisms from outside, but it is also intended to have a conciliatory purpose within the church, in which disputes continued between Jewish Christians, who insisted that Gentile Christians should be circumcised and keep the law, and Gentile Christians, who argued for a law-free faith.

4. Throughout Acts Luke seizes the opportunity to show to all who may read it that the Christian faith and witness are *not contrary to the laws and true interests of Judaism or of the Roman state*. There is thus a secondary apologetic purpose, but it is probably intended to provide Christians with weapons for their own defence of the faith rather than to speak directly to critical and hostile outsiders.

5. Finally, the church is shown to have *a continuing obligation to witness* to the messiah, regardless of the success of the mission. Acts, in its position alongside the Gospel, demonstrates that Christian witness to Jesus is part of the 'given basis' of the new religion. Luke is showing how witness confirms the status of Jesus, how it is justified by God's clear guidance, and how it remains binding on the church. The witness to Jesus is to be carried to 'the ends of the earth', a phrase which points beyond Rome; the picture at the end of Acts 28 is of an unfinished task. At the same time Luke is doubtless reminding the church that the pattern for its witness is to be seen in the life of the first Christians, which was itself modelled on the witness of Jesus himself.

Such a broadly-based purpose suggests that (as we might very reasonably expect) the church for which Luke was writing had a variety of needs. We do wrong to restrict Luke's purpose to one particular objective. Even the topic of witness, which I have proposed as comprehending much of Luke's purpose, must not be pressed too hard as the only topic of Acts.

Further Reading

H. Conzelmann, *The Theology of St Luke* (London: Faber, 1960).

P.J. Esler, *Community and Gospel in Luke–Acts* (Cambridge: Cambridge University Press, 1987).

E.A. Judge, *The Social Pattern of Christian Groups in the First Century* (London: Tyndale Press, 1960).

R. Maddox, *The Purpose of Luke–Acts* (Edinburgh: T. & T. Clark, 1982).

M.C. Parsons, *The Departure of Jesus in Luke–Acts* (JSNTSup, 21; Sheffield: JSOT Press, 1987).

W.C. van Unnik, 'The "book of Acts" the Confirmation of the Gospel', *NovT* 4 (1960), pp. 26-59; reprinted in *Sparsa Collecta* (Leiden: Brill, 1973), I, pp. 340-73.

P.W. Walaskay, *'And so we Came to Rome': The Political Perspective of St Luke* (Cambridge: Cambridge University Press, 1983).

3

THE WITNESS
OF THE CHURCH
TO THE MESSIAH

Acts as a Theological Work

AMONG THE GAINS OF SCHOLARSHIP in the latter half of the twenti-
eth century is the increasing recognition that the New Testament is
pre-eminently a *theological* book, in the sense that the main interest ot
its authors is to discuss topics that are theological, whether they are
writing in the outward form of a letter or something like a biography.
In fact, all of the authors were 'theologians' in the sense that they held
to a set of theological beliefs which found expression in their writings,
whether deliberately or unconsciously. And, finally, there is considerable variety in the theological positions of the different writers.

These insights have lent fresh interest to the study of the Gospels,
where the varying theological positions of the four Evangelists have
become the centre of interest. No book entitled 'A Theology of the
New Testament' is worthy of its name if it does not devote sections to
the individual Evangelists instead of simply using their writings as
sources for the teaching of Jesus.

What is true of the Gospels is equally true of Acts. The question
which is undoubtedly at the centre of contemporary study of Acts, and
which is probably the most interesting and useful, is the nature and
content of its theology. If Luke's hand can be seen so clearly in the
style and purpose of the book, it follows that its theological colouring
is due to him. Hence questions arise as to the character of this theology and as to its place in the history of early Christian thinking. Was
Luke a deep and creative thinker with a distinctive theology of his
own? Was he merely recording the theology of the early church, or

was he developing insights of his own in the course of his work? Was
he a close disciple of Paul, and does he share his theological outlook?
With what other areas of early Christianity does he have affinities?

The fact that Luke has a theological mind of his own is evident
from the way in which from time to time he makes explicit theological comments on the situation. He has his own forms of words for
summing up the preaching of the missionaries (e.g. Acts 9.22; 17.3;
18.5, 28) and other aspects of the experience of the church (Acts 4.31;
13.52). Moreover, the kind of things that Luke says in his own comments fit in closely with what the chief characters say in the remarks
and discourses attributed to them. This suggests to most scholars that,
whatever traditional basis Luke had for the various theological utter-
ances which he records, the final wording and theological outlook are
due to himself.

But what kind of theology is it? One can trace a distinctive, admittedly dynamic and developing, theology in the letters of Paul which
has certain characteristics that differentiate it from other theological
expressions in the NT. Equally there is a Johannine theology, or a
theology of the Letter to the Hebrews and so on. We need to ask
whether there is a Lukan theology in the same kind of way. Luke may
not have a theology except in the sense that he has picked up what he
was taught without doing anything creative with it himself. Or again
Luke may not have a unified and coherent theology at all. So is there a
'shape' or a distinctive motivation to be found in Luke's theology in
Acts?

The Delay of the Parousia

I will begin to answer this question by returning to consider again the
proposal which inaugurated modern study of Luke's theology, namely,
H. Conzelmann's identification of the main motivation for Luke's
work as being the delay of the parousia. That is to say, Conzelmann
isolated a motive in the light of which he believed that he could
demonstrate the distinctiveness of Lukan theology. He believed that
the theology of Luke–Acts as a whole was the result of a church and
an author trying to come to terms with the experience of disappointment: the church had expected that the Son of man would return,
as promised, and when with the passage of time this hope became
increasingly weak, the church was forced to rewrite its theology to fit

an extended period of time. So, where the future hope had originally been the factor that shaped and controlled theology, its function was taken over by the presence of the Holy Spirit, and where the present time had been essentially one of waiting for the coming parousia, it now subtly changed its character and became one of service and mission. The future hope did not evaporate completely, but the object of hope was now so remote that present action came to replace it. Thus right at the outset of Acts the disciples who ask when the kingdom is to be restored to Israel are told not to fill their minds with questions to which God alone has the answer, but rather to be witnesses to the world in the power of the Spirit. And where the early church originally waited joyously for the parousia and was filled with excitement at the prospect, now it is depicted as drawing its inspiration from the presence and power of the Spirit.

Such is the theory. Its weaknesses have been frequently exposed, but it remains significant because it forced scholars to recognize that there was a theological puzzle to be solved and made them come up with a better solution. Among the critical questions to be asked of it are these:

1. *To what extent was the church initially dominated by the hope of the parousia of the Son of man?* There is a strong case that, as far back as we can trace its message, the church was concerned at least as much with the death and resurrection of Jesus. Certainly this is the case in Paul, whose summary of the gospel is concerned with these matters and who is here relying on what is generally regarded as early tradition (1 Cor. 15.3-5). Even in 1 Thessalonians, where there is considerable emphasis on waiting for the parousia, the heart of the gospel is still the fact that Christ died for believers and rose (1 Thess. 4.14; 5.9-10). This letter in fact gives a balance between past event and future expectation at an early point in Paul's career.

2. *At what point in its history did the church experience the so-called 'delay' of the parousia?* Was it a matter of months or years? Was there indeed a period of crisis and disappointment at all, or was the church perhaps always aware of the need for a period of waiting? Writers earlier than Luke, such as Paul, appear to have been well aware that the parousia would not necessarily happen immediately. Even if there were heightened expectations of the end of the world as a a result of such events as the fall of Jerusalem in 70 CE and a consequent sense of disappointment when nothing happened thereafter, the kind of outlook which is found in Acts had developed much earlier. To

suggest that Luke was the first NT writer to express Christian theology in this way is to misunderstand the writers who preceded him.

3. *How far did the church's experience of the Spirit and its activity in mission have a different role in the early days from what they had in Luke's day?* That is to say, where is the evidence that the Spirit and the mission were given a different significance or a different emphasis from what they originally had in order to compensate for the decline of the hope of the parousia? The evidence points the other way. The activity of the Spirit in the church as the sign of divine presence and power again goes back to Paul's earliest letters and is something that is taken for granted (1 Thess. 1.5; 4.8; 5.19; Gal. 3.2-5; 4.6; 5.16-25). Equally, the fact of mission is crystal clear in Paul's earliest writings. 1 Thessalonians is the self-conscious expression of a missionary whose concern is to proclaim the good news, win converts and enable them to continue, and Galatians is the story of one who was called to proclaim Christ among the Gentiles. There is doubtless a close relationship between the Spirit and the coming Lord, but there is nothing to indicate that the Spirit and mission had any significantly different role in Acts from that which they had in the historical experience of Paul or in any traditions that we can isolate behind his writings.

These points are sufficient to show that the need to rewrite the church's theology did not exist in the time of Luke; whatever needed to be done had already been done. It follows that the 'shape' of Luke's theology is not determined by this factor. Nevertheless, before leaving it we should note that it has called to our attention the significance of the Spirit and mission in the life of the church, and we should be asking whether this throws any light on Luke's theology.

'Early Catholicism' and Third Generation Theology

A number of scholars have raised the question whether Acts is to be understood as a document of 'early catholicism'. Here we are dealing with the suggestion that Luke is writing as a second-generation or third-generation Christian who is unconsciously writing a theology for a church which is no longer characterized by pristine enthusiasm, but by its development into a fairly rigid institution in which rules and regulations and organization have largely replaced the spontaneity of an earlier body dominated by the Spirit. Luke's work, therefore, is to be placed not so much alongside earlier Christian documents as rather alongside the writings of the second century. In these we see the body of believers developing into the so-called 'early catholic' church, with its characteristic emphasis on the institution based on fixed traditions handed down from the earlier days, legitimating itself by its succession from the apostles, and providing for a long and settled existence in the world by the development of fixed forms of ministry and ritual. On this view Luke would be contributing to the development of the church's self-understanding by bringing out those elements which helped to undergird this particular view.

E. Käsemann is probably the most influential advocate of this understanding of Acts. Writing on Acts 19.1-7, he says that the narrative

> betrays, in common with all those allied to it, an ideological theology of history. Its characteristic feature is this: it reads back into the past as an historical reality the postulate of an *Una sancta* grounded on the apostolic fellowship and then, conversely, uses this postulate to validate the claims of the orthodox Church of his own times. Luke has overpainted and reshaped history in order to defend the *Una sancta apostolica* against the assault of the Gnostics and other heretics of his day. We can only understand him as an historian, if we have first understood him as a theologian. As a theologian he can only be understood from his doctrine of a legitimate Church (*Essays*, p. 148).

However, this interpretation of the underlying motivation of Luke's theology in Acts has rightly fallen into disfavour among recent commentators. It is pointed out that, apart from Acts 20.17-38, Luke shows very little interest in the organization of the church and its ministry and leadership. He is not interested in any kind of apostolic succession from the past, nor does he lay down what is to be done in the future. Even the motif of heresy, which became prominent with the rise of Gnosticism, is scarcely prominent, and certainly the threat of Gnosticism itself is outside the author's horizon. Nor is it correct to say that the primitive enthusiasm and freedom have dwindled away. Above all, there is no sense in which the church has moved to the centre of the stage and replaced the Word of God or placed it under its control.

H. Conzelmann (Keck and Martyn [eds.], *Studies in Luke–Acts*, pp. 305-307) attempts a different explanation. Luke belongs consciously to the 'third generation'. Underlying Luke's presentation of his story is the way in which he distinguishes the period of the apostles from that of their followers and uses the latter as a bridge between the apostles and his own day. Thus the concept of the 'twelve apostles' is developed, while Paul, who belongs to the second generation, necessarily does not belong in the apostolic circle but acts as a link between it and the writer's own time. What we have, then, is 'third generation' theology rather than early catholicism. And this theology stresses the links with the past through its careful structuring of history into periods and through its concept of tradition.

Conzelmann's structuring of Christian history into three generations is rather too neat. The important element in his theory is that it highlights the significance of the Twelve. They are associated with the origin of the church, and they disappear from sight once their role has been fulfilled; they are no longer seen after Acts 15. Yet for Luke they are tied to the church in Jerusalem in its early days. Historically they were not the agents of mission outside its immediate environs, and to that extent their importance is relative. The reason why Luke is not interested in them after Acts 15 is not that the initial period of the church is now past, but that the future of the church lay with those like Paul who were prepared to take the gospel to the ends of the earth.

Conzelmann's view that Luke was writing an account of the beginnings of Christianity is articulated in the specific form that Luke was '*historicizing the kerygma*', a phrase which appears to mean that Luke was turning from the concept of the gospel as a message, with existential significance which had to be proclaimed, to telling a piece of history which now formed part of world history and was being objectified as a basis for belief. Luke's purpose, then, was to take the Christian message and to give it its place in the ongoing process of 'salvation history'.

In this particular form, the theory is open to question. The existence of 'salvation-historical' thinking at earlier stages in the NT church has been demonstrated by O. Cullmann (*Salvation in History*). From the beginning, the 'kerygma' was concerned with the historical facts of the coming, death and resurrection of Jesus and with the existential significance of these facts. There never was a time when the heart of Christianity was a message with no firm ties to history. The view that Luke changed an existential message into a historical narrative is thus based on the mistaken assumption that prior to Luke the story of Jesus was not related as the basis of the kerygma. And, of course, it is clear that the Christian message proclaimed by the witnesses in Acts is meant to contain an existential challenge for Luke's readers.

But the suggestion that Luke was deliberately telling the story of

Christian beginnings is fruitful. To the best of our knowledge, Luke was the only person to tell a story that linked together the ministry of Jesus with the growth of the church. It is true that Matthew and Mark have an ecclesiastical dimension to their Gospels in that they bring out the significance of the story *for* the church, but they do not tell the story *of* the church, even if some of its experiences may be reflected in the narrative. Equally, although John appears to work on two levels, so that his Jesus speaks at one and the same time as the earthly Jesus and the exalted Lord, the story does not extend beyond the Easter events, and even the giving of the Spirit is treated as part of the story of Jesus.

But Luke goes beyond this. The story of Jesus is incomplete without the story of the church. There is a point of separation between them, the cut-off point being the ascension of Jesus, but they form one story. (Here again Conzelmann detected a significant point, but misinterpreted it as indicating a three-part analysis of salvation history as a whole into the periods of Israel, Jesus and the Church, rather than a two-part analysis into the periods of promise and fulfilment, with the latter period containing the life of Jesus and the mission of the church.) The vital point is the bringing together of the two stories and the careful links that are forged between them in a variety of ways.

Why did Luke bring them together? The two parts are linked together by promise and fulfilment, by type and antitype, by command and obedience. Luke, we may say, had the insight to recognize that the Jesus story was incomplete; it pointed forward to and demanded the church. Or, to put it otherwise, the church is shown how it necessarily developed out of the Jesus story. Hence the question of the theological shape of Acts is part of the question of the theological shape of Luke–Acts as a whole.

If we ask the question as to why Luke felt it necessary to write his own Gospel when other 'attempts' to do so already existed, the answer must be partly that Luke's dissatisfaction with the other Gospels was they did not tell the whole story which he conceived to be necessary in a full account of Christian beginnings (I.H. Marshall, 'Luke and his "Gospel"'). He wanted to write a 'complete' account of the basis of Christianity. A church with only a 'Gospel' like that of Mark as its foundation document was lacking in credentials. So it was not the case that Luke conceived the idea of writing a Gospel and then thought that it would be a good idea to carry the story further. On the contrary, he believed that the right way to deal with the problems discussed in the previous chapter was to write a work which would record both the story of Jesus and the story of the early church.

It should be noted in passing that to do this was in no way to relativize the position of Jesus. F. Overbeck was quite mistaken when he wrote, 'Nothing is more instructive for the Lukan conception of evangelical history, insofar as he sees in it a topic for historical writing, than his idea of adding Acts to the Gospel as its continuation. This is an act of tactlessness of world-historical dimensions, the greatest excess of the false position which presents itself to Luke as an object' (*Christentum und Kultur* [1919], p. 78). Quite the contrary. The whole purpose of Acts is to add to the witness to Jesus already presented in part in the Gospel. Overbeck's comment is unjust to Luke and decisively fails to understand what he was doing.

It would seem that Luke had at least two motives for what he did. On the one hand, he wished to give Theophilus and those like him some backing and confirmation for the Christian message which they had already heard. He recognized that simply telling the story of Jesus was inadequate for this purpose. On the other hand, it is hard to avoid the impression that in so doing Luke was placing before the church of his own day the challenge posed by its roots. He was reminding the church of its marching orders. The stress on witness in Acts has a twofold thrust. On the one hand, it contains the testimony to Jesus which helps to confirm the message heard by converts, and, on the other hand, it reminds the church of its responsibility to maintain that witness for the future.

Did Luke, then, see the history which he recorded as that of a period separate from his own time, a golden age in the past, a pattern to imitate, a period from which the church had declined? Acts 20 might suggest this, with its Pauline vision of a church about to be ravaged by dangerous wolves once he was no longer there to protect it. Yet this is the only place in Acts where this anxiety is expressed, and it must be remembered that the church in Acts is not free from weakness and sinfulness. We should beware, therefore, of seeing an absolute division between the period of the early church and that of Luke's church in his thinking, but to say this is obviously not to deny that one of Luke's purposes was to remind the church of its foundation and to call it back to basics.

So we find ourselves moving to the position that the shape of Acts is determined at least in part by the need to provide the church with its credentials, to set its course for the future. Bengel aptly saw the significance of Acts in his final comment in his commentary on the last verse: *Habes, Ecclesia, formam tuam: tuum est, servare eam, et depositum custodire* (Here, O church, you have your pattern: it is your task to preserve it and to guard what has been entrusted to you). These words, which are reminiscent of motifs in the Pastoral Epistles, are a fair summary of one of the functions of Acts. Luke's theology is shaped by the need to give to the church of his day a statement of the gospel and an incentive to proclaim it.

The question then arises as to how far any Lukan bias is at work in this presentation. Clearly, Luke could have idealized the early days of the church in order to make it appear as a worthy pattern to be followed. Equally he could have emphasized certain elements and underemphasized or ignored others. Literary considerations could have led to a structuring which was not in accord with historical reality. How far is the theology presented that of Luke himself, giving no doubt what he imagined to be the teaching of the early Christians? To answer these questions it is necessary to sketch in some of the content of Luke's theology.

The Content and Nature of the Witness

The previous chapter has suggested that the theme of witness to Jesus is what shapes the theology of Acts, and I have suggested further that witness has two aspects—the content of the witness and the character of the witnesses. Provided that we do not interpret these two categories too rigidly, we have here the 'shape' of the theology of Acts which will be considered further in the remainder of this chapter and in the next chapter. The discussion will be organized somewhat loosely in the present section around the content of the witness and in the next chapter around the character and function of the witnesses.

1. The first thing that we note is that the theology of Acts is frequently presented in the form of preaching or as *kerygma*. That is to say, one of the vehicles which Luke employs is the speech. Doubtless this reflects the historical fact that the early Christian missionaries were preachers. At the same time also there is an obvious basis for the use of speeches in the historical genre of Acts. Nevertheless, the form is theologically significant. While recent scholarship has emphasized

that Acts as a whole is using the category of 'story' to present the
author's theological message, Luke focuses that message in the speeches.
These speeches were intended as a medium of persuasion. The
recognized purpose of the speech in the ancient world was to influence
people; some responded positively, others ignored what was said, and
yet others responded with antagonism. There is therefore an element
of reasoned argument in the speeches.

2. For Acts the decisive point in the debate with the Jews is *whether
Jesus is the messiah*, the future ruler and deliverer prophesied in the
Scriptures as was understood by Jews at that time. Side by side with
this understanding of the significance of Jesus is the title of *Lord*. This
is a term which Luke has already used extensively in the Gospel in
order to refer to Jesus. It is used with great frequency in Acts. One
effect of the usage is that a certain ambiguity arises since the same
Greek word is also used to refer to God the Father (e.g. in Acts 2.34,
in the quotation from Ps. 110.1, the first occurrence of the word
refers to God, whereas the second occurrence ['my Lord'] refers to
the Psalmist's 'master', who is taken to be the messiah and then identified with Jesus). This juxtaposition of uses of the same word with
reference to God and with reference to Jesus may well have resulted
in the readers seeing Jesus in an authoritative position similar to that
of God.

This dual status as messiah and Lord is regarded as being made
manifest through the resurrection and the gift of the Spirit. The
argument in Acts 2.22-36 shows that Psalm 110 was regarded as
fulfilled in the resurrection and ascension of Jesus, and therefore the
title of 'Lord' used there is to be regarded as belonging to Jesus; and
the outpouring of the Spirit is understood as being the work of Jesus
who has received the Spirit from the Father. This is presumably to be
taken to imply that Jesus shares the sovereign status of the Father and
hence is to be understood as the Lord. Luke himself comments that the
teaching of the witnesses was intended to show that Jesus was the
messiah (Acts 17.3; 18.5).

Other categories are used to explain more fully the position and
significance of Jesus. The prophecy of Moses that God would raise up
a *prophet* like himself is said to be fulfilled in Jesus (Acts 3.22-23).
Here similarly the basis for the claim is that Jesus was known to have
done the kind of things that prophets did and to have had a prophetic
self-consciousness—as the Gospel of Luke indicates. Hence Jesus is

regarded as having an authority like that of Moses. Jesus is also spoken of as *God's servant* (Acts 3.13, 26; 4.30) with special reference to the description in Isaiah 53 (cf. Acts 8.32-33). It is instructive that, without further explanation, the reference of this passage is not clear to one of its readers—is the prophet perhaps referring to himself, and if not, to whom (Acts 8.34-35)? And the fact that Isaiah 53.7-8 is read gives a first-class opportunity for showing how the details of the prophecy correspond with the details of the trial and death of Jesus. This is a good example of where the reference of a prophetic passage is a matter of debate, but appeal to the match between it and the experiences of Jesus is considered sufficient to make the point.

The title of *Son* is used only twice. Luke associates it with the preaching of Paul (Acts 9.20), and in Paul's speech in Pisidian Antioch it is found in a quotation from Ps. 2.7 (Acts 13.33). The origins of the appeal to the Psalm are shrouded in obscurity. There is no attempt by Paul to argue that the Psalm must apply to Jesus. Rather, it is likely that the combined beliefs that Jesus was the Son of God (based, among other things, on his own reported self-understanding) and that he had been raised from the dead led to an appropriation of the Psalm as testimony to him, since resurrection could easily be seen under the metaphor of 'begetting'. Thus the Psalm is used more as a vehicle of proclamation than as a means of proof of the status of Jesus.

3. From his status we turn to the question of *what Jesus does*. He now functions as a Saviour, the Author of Life (Acts 3.15; 5.31). This position is related to the fact that by God's plan he was put to death and raised to life.

Debate continues on whether his life-giving function is something assigned to him by God in and through raising him from the dead, or whether it also rests in some way upon his death. That Luke knows that his death has a saving significance is plain from Luke 22.19-20 and Acts 20.28, and it may be implicit in the identification of Jesus as the Servant of Yahweh. Yet it is curious that the motifs of Christ dying 'for us' and 'for our sins' are not found in the preaching in Acts, even though it would seem that these were fixed motifs in the early preaching attested in Paul and elsewhere.

The position of Jesus is such that his *Name* is now powerful, in the same way as the 'Name' of the Father himself is powerful. This enables his followers to do the same kind of mighty works as he did in his lifetime—but always as his agents who call on his name in order to do so (e.g. Acts 3.6, 16; 4.30; 16.18). Further, his status is such that he can confer forgiveness, the gift of the Spirit, and salvation (e.g. Acts 2.38; 10.43; 22.16).

The resurrection is also seen as the guarantee that he will act in the future as the judge (Acts 17.31). Presumably the argument is that the only person known to have been resurrected is appropriately qualified to act as judge. He will come at some future point to act as judge of the living and the dead and to inaugurate the 'universal restoration' (Acts 3.20-21; 10.42).

4. A central element in the structure of the speeches is their appeal to Scriptural *prophecy*, whereby on the one hand certain prophetic passages are seen to have come to fulfilment in contemporary events, and on the other hand the significance of certain events is seen in that they fulfil prophecy. The 'proof' is generally developed by implying that there is an obvious match between the event described in the prophecy and the contemporary event, and that no other known event fits the prophecy. Thus, in Acts 2.25-32 it is considered self-evident that in Psalm 16 David (the putative author) is speaking about deliverance from death; but this prophecy finds its counterpart in the resurrection of Jesus—which is assumed as a historical fact by the preacher—and in no other event, and manifestly not in the case of David himself, whose tomb was there for all to see. The fact that Jesus rose from the dead is not proved by reference to prophecy, but by the testimony of witnesses; the fact that the messiah was not to be held in death is shown from Scripture, and the correspondence between the two facts is used to establish that Jesus is the messiah. Then the appeal is made to the audience to respond to the message.

From this we can see that prophecy is used to indicate the status of Jesus, and the messianic role is filled out in numerous ways. The role of the OT in Luke–Acts has been discussed by D.L. Bock, who has defended the view that Luke uses a 'proclamation from prophecy and pattern' method, and elaborates on this by saying that 'Luke sees the Scripture fulfilled in Jesus in terms of the fulfilment of OT prophecy and in terms of the reintroduction and fulfilment of the OT patterns that point to the presence of God's saving work' (D.L. Bock, *Proclamation*, p. 274). Bock also claims that Luke's purpose in this is 'to calm any doubts that may have existed in the church about either Jesus' position in the plan of God or his offering of God's salvation to

all men, especially the direct offer of salvation to the Gentiles'
(*Proclamation*, p. 279).

5. Alongside prophecy, the theme of *witness* is prominent. Witness
is significant because it is clear that the facts about the career of Jesus
must be attested if the proof from prophecy is to work. A Jewish
stress on the need to corroborate claims by eyewitness testimony may
be present. Hence there is a strong stress on the place of the Twelve as
the people who have witnessed (and can therefore bear testimony to)
the main events in the career of Jesus, including especially his death
and resurrection and the pouring out of the Spirit. However, the task
of witness is not confined to the Twelve. The personal experience of
the living power of Christ by other Christians entitles them equally to
be regarded as witnesses, even though they are not eyewitnesses of the
foundation events.

6. Witness is ideally something which is to be believed and accepted.
Acts is concerned above all with the evangelistic function of witness.
At the same time, it is something that takes place *in a hostile and
antagonistic environment*. It is to be undertaken whether or not it will
lead to conversion. It is necessary that testimony is borne to Jesus
before all classes and kinds of people. The point is that there can now
no longer be any appeal to ignorance. There may have been in the
past, but now it is not possible in light of the clear witness that has
been heard (Acts 17.30; cf. 3.17).

7. This leads on to a consideration of *the people to whom the witness is offered*. In the writings of Paul it is fundamental that 'all have
sinned', both Jews and Gentiles, and need to be reconciled to God on
the basis of the death of Jesus. Luke holds essentially the same standpoint. Right from the outset it is clear that all people are called to
acknowledge Jesus as messiah and Lord. The Jews generally are characterized as a 'corrupt generation' (Acts 2.40), and their 'wicked
ways' (Acts 3.26) and sinfulness culminate in the killing of Jesus (Acts
2.23). The people as a whole seem to be understood as accessories to
his death unless they dissociate themselves by repentance and baptism.
Their sin can be regarded as due to ignorance (Acts 3.17), but they
still need to repent and to be baptised in order to have their sins wiped
out (Acts 3.19; cf. 22.16). Repentance and faith expressed in baptism
are the required human attitudes (Acts 20.21). The word 'salvation'
can be used to summarize what is offered in and through Jesus, and it
apparently needs no explanation (Acts 4.12). Moreover, Jesus is the

only agent through whom salvation is possible. The preaching of the apostles is designed to offer repentance and forgiveness to Israel (Acts 5.31). Cornelius, a devout God-fearing person, welcomes the gospel, and it may be significant that Peter's address to him refers to the function of Jesus as judge and speaks of belief in him as the means of forgiveness (Acts 10.42-43). When preaching to Jews in the Dispersion, Paul similarly preaches that forgiveness is offered through Jesus, and people are set free from the sins from which they could not be freed by the law of Moses. Rejection of this message leads to loss of eternal life (Acts 13.39, 46). In a Gentile context, the people are urged to turn from 'worthless things' to the living God (Acts 14.15) and to repent, since God no longer overlooks human ignorance (Acts 17.30-31). 'Salvation' is the content of the message (Acts 16.17, 30-31).

It is fair to conclude from this that Luke regards all people, both Jews and Gentiles, as in need of a salvation that comes only through Jesus. Piety, such as that shown by Cornelius the Roman centurion (Acts 10.2), is an indication of readiness to accept the message, and is pleasing to God (Acts 10.31), but is no substitute for actually responding to the gospel, which brings salvation (Acts 11.14, 18).

8. How does Luke see *the effects of response to the message?* Its purpose is to lead people (a) to avoid the judgment which would otherwise come upon them; (b) to experience salvation in a positive sense; and (c) to join the company of people who know this experience. These three items are variously stressed in the preaching in Acts. Acknowledging that Jesus is the messiah and the source of life leads to reception of salvation. Luke uses terms like salvation and eternal life to express the results of belief.

Characteristics of Luke's Christology

We can now try to draw some conclusions about the characteristics of this theology:

1. The Christology is presented in terms of the exaltation of a *man* (Acts 2.22; 17.31) to Lordship (Acts 2.36; 3.13; 5.31). This could lead us to suppose that Luke has a Christology in which Jesus, a human being, has the status of lordship conferred on him by God at his exaltation. In that case we would have to ask what kind of status is assigned to Jesus during his earthly life. Luke, however, certainly understands Jesus as being from his birth the Son of God (Lk. 1.35),

and he also refers to him in the Gospel as 'the Lord' (e.g. Lk. 2.11; 7.13; 24.34). Therefore, in a passage like Acts 2.36, the force for Luke is rather that the exaltation confirms the existing status of Jesus in a kind of public announcement.

Luke says nothing directly about the pre-existence of Jesus as the Son of God. It is not clear whether this omission is simply due to the kind of presentation which is being offered. The speeches in Acts are concerned to show how the wicked deed of those who crucified Jesus was reversed by God who raised him from the dead. This was an appropriate starting point for speaking to a Jewish audience, since it started from facts that they could easily grasp. To have started by saying 'God sent his Son into the world, but you put him to death' would have been to start in quite the wrong place, since the idea of a Son whom God could send into the world would have been outside their comprehension. That is to say, the setting of Luke's christological statements in speeches to Jews made any reference to the pre-existence of the messiah inappropriate. When divine sonship is mentioned, it is in connection with the resurrection (Acts 13.33).

Also missing from Acts is any reference to the kind of understanding of the present status of Jesus expressed by Paul when he talks in terms of believers being united with Christ, or being 'in Christ', where Christ is conceived of as a cosmic spiritual figure with whom each believer may be joined. Rather for Luke Jesus is a living being who can speak directly to people (Acts 9.4-6) and appear to them in visions (Acts 18.9; 23.11; cf. 27.23-24 of an angel of God) and to whom one can pray (Acts 7.59).

These points show that the Christology which Luke actually expresses lacks the profundity of Paul or John. They may suggest that its character is pre-Pauline rather than post-Pauline. The evidence of other NT writers shows that the titles of Christ, Lord and Son of God were current from as early a date as we can trace. Such terms as 'author of life' and 'leader' (Acts 3.15; 5.31) are rarely found elsewhere in the NT (Heb. 2.10; 12.2), and there is no way of telling whether they are primitive. The emphasis on the exaltation of Jesus fits in quite appropriately into the early preaching of the church, with its concern to vindicate the position of the One who had been rejected and crucified.

2. It is noteworthy that Luke says next to nothing in Acts about the significance of the death of Jesus—other than that it was God's will

that he should be put to death by wicked people before being exalted. Through Jesus people may gain forgiveness of sins, but apart from Acts 20.28—in an address to elders of the church—the place of the death of Jesus for believers and for their sins is ignored, although it appears to have functioned in the primitive preaching. Even if the thought is implicit in the understanding of Jesus as the Servant of Yahweh, it is still not expressed explicitly. Why is it that the concept does not function actively in Acts—especially in an evangelistic context? It may be noted that Paul also can sum up the way to salvation without reference to the cross in Rom. 10.9. In 1 Thess. 1.9-10, which probably reflects missionary preaching, the status of Jesus as the Son of God who will come from heaven is linked to his having been raised from the dead. Again, the stress in Phil. 2.6-11 lies on the exaltation of Jesus to be Lord. These texts suggest that there was more than one pattern of evangelistic preaching in the early church, and that Luke has followed one such pattern perhaps because he wished to stress the lordship and messiahship of Jesus in relation to the Jews. It is likely that the full force of the significance of the death of Jesus did not develop immediately after Easter, and that the church's initial preaching was taken up with what would have been seen as the stupendous fact of the resurrection. The initial question in witness to Jews was the messiahship of Jesus. Again, therefore, we have a clue to the primitive nature of the Christology in Acts.

3. Finally, the concept of witness by the apostles to the resurrection is expressed in language that is somewhat distinctive of Luke, although it is not without echoes elsewhere in the NT. It is clearly present in 1 Cor. 15.3-5, where this concept (though not the actual word 'witness') is closely associated with the apostolic message. But at the same time the prominence of the concept in Acts and the way in which it is used may indicate that Luke has developed it in his own manner.

The evidence is thus by no means unanimous that Luke has imposed his own theology on the early Christian church. Simply to claim that he is deliberately 'archaizing' is hardly an argument, unless it can be shown that the language used cannot be that of the early church. To seek refuge, on the other hand, in the claim that, since we know so little about the earliest preaching of the church, Luke's picture cannot be falsified is also somewhat weak. Yet it remains probable that Luke has given a fair picture of the themes of the early church, often based on traditional material, but not without some contribution of his own.

Further Reading

D.L. Bock, *Proclamation from Prophecy and Pattern: Lucan Old Testament Christology* (JSNTSup, 12; Sheffield: JSOT Press, 1987).

H. Conzelmann, *The Theology of St Luke* (London: Faber, 1960).

O. Cullmann, *Salvation in History* (London: SCM Press, 1967).

E. Käsemann, 'The Disciples of John the Baptist in Ephesus', in *Essays on New Testament Themes* (London: SCM Press, 1964), pp. 136-48.

I.H. Marshall, 'Luke and his "Gospel"', in P. Stuhlmacher (ed.), *The Gospel and the Gospels* (Grand Rapids: Eerdmans, 1991), pp. 272-92.

4

THE WITNESSING
COMMUNITY
AND ITS PROBLEMS

THE THEOLOGICAL MESSAGE OF ACTS finds expression not only in the content of the witness borne to Jesus Christ, but also in the teaching which is implicit in the story of the witnesses and the witnessing community. The nature of the church and the problems and issues which it faced form a major part of the theological agenda of Acts.

The Witnesses

We can identify three categories of witness. First, Acts begins with the appointment of the apostles to be witnesses. So significant is their task that the first incident reported in Acts is the appointment of a twelfth member of the apostolic group to take the place of Judas. The task of the Twelve is to bear witness to Jesus, and the qualification that they must have been with Jesus all the time that he was with his disciples indicates that their witness included testimony to his earthly career and teaching.

Secondly, specific individuals have the task of witness. Stephen and Paul are both so called, although neither of them belonged to this group (Acts 22.15, 20). Certainly Paul could bear testimony to the resurrected Jesus (Acts 22.14-15), and it may be that the same is true of Stephen, who testified to seeing the Son of man (Acts 7.56). Although the group is not explicitly widened to cover disciples in general, in Acts 8.4 and 11.19-20 the activity of proclaiming the Word is attributed to those who were not apostles, and even to people from Cyprus and Cyrene. Therefore it can probably be concluded that the number of witnesses was not closed, even though the number of the Twelve was fixed.

Thirdly, God himself is said to bear witness to Jesus by the gift of the Spirit and by doing signs and wonders through the evangelists (Acts 14.3; 15.8).

From this we see that there is a distinction in Luke's mind between the roles of the Twelve and of those who came after them. For Luke, the facts concerning the life of Jesus—'all that he did both in Judaea and in Jerusalem' (Acts 10.39)—and his resurrection were of crucial importance, and therefore he stresses the role of the Twelve as the people best fitted to bear authoritative witness to these facts, both in order to establish them historically, and to indicate their significance. It is the apostles who stand at the fountainhead of the tradition recorded in the Gospel (Lk. 1.2). Luke, therefore, emphasizes that the original witnesses were appointed by divine choice in view of their crucial role in God's plan of salvation. (There could in theory have been a larger number—Joseph and Matthias were a 'shortlist' out of a larger number of candidates for the post of twelfth man—but the divine choice restricted the total to twelve.) Neither Stephen nor Paul—nor other Christians—could function in this way, since they had not been with Jesus during his earthly life or been present at the original resurrection appearances; but they could bear witness to the fact of the resurrected Lord and proclaim its significance. And so too could other Christians after them.

The Power for Witness

Luke sets up no explicit contrast between the law and the Spirit, such as is found in the writings of Paul (Rom. 7.6). Some scholars have detected an implicit allusion to Ps. 68.18 in Acts 2.33, where a Psalm which was taken in Judaism to refer to the gift of the law is now applied to the gift of the Spirit. Whether or not this is so, certainly the Spirit occupies an integral place in the theology of Luke.

Right at the beginning, the coming of the Holy Spirit upon the disciples is interpreted as power for witness to Jesus, and the Pentecost event is seen as a fulfilment of the prophecy of baptism with the Holy Spirit. The initial group of disciples (all 120 of them are probably meant) receive the Spirit, and the event is marked by their bursting into praise of God in various languages. This is interpreted as one of the signs of the last days, and it is significant that the Spirit is now given to 'all flesh'.

Thereafter the Spirit is continually active in the church. We have a string of passages in which people are filled with the Spirit before speaking publicly as witnesses to Christ, and the Spirit is regarded as witnessing along with the human actors (Acts 5.32). Some Christians are described as 'being filled' with, or 'full of', the Spirit, in contrast to the texts which speak of a person 'receiving a filling' before a specific act of witness (for the former: Acts 6.3, 5; 11.24; for the latter: Acts 2.4; 4.8; 9.17; 13.9). Various other phrases are used—the Spirit 'comes upon' people, is 'poured out' upon them, is 'received' by them, 'falls upon' them. Further, the Spirit gives direction to the church or to the witnesses (e.g. Acts 8.29; 10.19; 13.2; 16.6-7; 20.23). In some cases this direction is given through prophets guided by the Spirit.

All this shows that the Spirit is given to the church in various ways for the purpose of mission, directing the work and giving the capacity to speak and even to do mighty works.

There is, however, a further set of passages where the Spirit is given to people at the point when they hear the gospel and are baptised with water or shortly afterwards (Acts 2.38; 8.14-19; 10.44-47; 11.15-16; 15.8; in 19.1-7, however, the 'disciples' had not previously received Christian baptism). Sometimes the laying on of hands is part of the process (Acts 8.18; 19.6). There are also places where the Spirit is with the church in a more general kind of way to strengthen it (Acts 9.31; 13.52).

In this second group of passages the Spirit functions to give testimony to the church of the reality of its experience, and the fact that the Spirit is given to Gentiles as well as Jews is of great importance in attesting that both groups of people are acceptable to God. So the presence of the Spirit is a sign to the recipients and to those who observe them that God is at work in their lives.

It would seem to follow from this that there were definite, observable signs of receiving the Spirit. In a number of places there is reference to speaking in other tongues (Acts 2.4; 10.46; 19.6), and this has led some scholars to conclude that this was the normal accompaniment of the gift of the Spirit.

Further, it has been argued that these occasions were often subsequent to the initial act of belief in Christ, and hence there has arisen the view that in Acts the reception of the gift of the Spirit may be an experience subsequent to conversion and distinct from it. Hence we have a so-called 'charismatic' interpretation of Acts in which the gift of the Spirit, accompanied by speaking in tongues, is a kind of 'second' stage in Christian experience subsequent to conversion (R. Stronstad, *The Charismatic Theology of St Luke*).

It has also been suggested that the Spirit in Acts is consistently and exclusively linked with the witness of the church, and is therefore to be understood as the divine provision for Christian witness rather than as what might be called one of the divine blessings associated with salvation. The Spirit in Acts is then seen as pre-eminently the 'Spirit of prophecy' activating the church for witness rather than as the agent of conversion and sanctification.

All this drives something of a wedge between Luke and Paul, since for the latter the Spirit is above all the divine gift bringing salvation and transforming the character of the converted. What are we to make of these various views?

1. Luke undoubtedly describes some events which cannot be regarded as 'normal' conversions, such as the cases of Cornelius (Acts 10) and the twelve men at Ephesus (Acts 19.1-7). It also seems likely that the case of the Samaritan converts (Acts 8.14-19) was unusual. We should not, therefore, regard these as materials for establishing a pattern. Rather Acts 2.38 would seem to set a pattern according to which repentance and baptism lead to forgiveness and the gift of the Spirit.

2. The reception of the Spirit appears to have been something that was usually recognizable and which therefore acted as assurance to the recipients of their new status and as confirmation to others that they were accepted by God. Doubtless, this could be regarded as part of the work of the Spirit in promoting the mission of the church, but this seems to be an unnecessarily restricted interpretation. It is better to say that the universal reception of the Spirit with its prophetic gifts is a sign of the new age.

3. We have to distinguish a number of separate actions of the Spirit. The same person can be filled with the Spirit more than once. Some people are singled out for mention as being (continually) full of the Spirit. But when allowance has been made for the special cases mentioned above, it is certainly the case that for Luke, as for Paul, reception of the Spirit is an essential part of Christian experience (Acts 19.2; Rom. 8.9). Thereafter, people may have repeated experiences

of being filled with the Spirit, usually for special acts of Christian witness or to convey experiences of joyfulness that strengthen their faith (Acts 4.31; 13.52).

It seems that a view which confines the experience of the Spirit in the theology of Acts to empowerment for witness and direction for mission is too narrow. The gift of the Spirit plays an important role in Christian assurance, just as it does in Paul. Luke is not concerned with the moral and spiritual changes in converts, and says very little about the role of the Spirit in this respect (but here Acts 11.24 may be significant). He knows that the Spirit is given to specific individuals for specific acts of witness and service. The important point which emerges is that the Spirit is given to all believers—and this gift includes empowering for witness.

Luke's teaching here certainly has loose ends and is 'untidy'. That may be inherent in the nature of the topic: the Spirit's working is not something that can be neatly categorized in a rational way but retains an element of the mysterious.

The Scope of the Witness

One of the major threads which runs through Acts is the way in which God is seen to direct the witness of the church towards the creation of a community composed of both Jews and Gentiles.

1. At the beginning the Twelve bear *witness to Jews*, implicitly to the so-called 'Hebrews'. By Acts 6 it is clear that the witness has also included so-called 'Hellenistic' Jews, distinguished from the former group by the fact that Greek was their only or preferred language over against Aramaic, with all that this implies regarding cultural characteristics.

2. It is a moot point whether *the speech of Stephen* in Acts 7 implies a wider scope for the witness. The criticism of temple worship is more an attack on a religious cult which allowed no room for God to work in new ways than an attack on the Jewish religion as a whole. Stephen is accused of speaking against Moses and the law, and his claim that the Jews themselves have failed to keep the law of Moses could be understood to imply that Christians are not opposed to it. Thus there is no indication of a turning against the Christians' Jewish heritage at

this point, and there is nothing to indicate that the Gentiles are in view, although it can be argued that theologically the ground has been cleared for witness to them.

3. But from this point a host of incidents indicate that *the scope is to be widened to include the Gentiles*:

a. The preaching of Philip in Samaria and the attendant conversions (Acts 8.4-25). This preaching is validated by Peter and John who shared in it (Acts 8.25).

b. The conversion of the Ethiopian official who is not a Jew and probably not a proselyte but rather a 'God-fearer' (Acts 8.26-40).

c. The conversion of Saul/Paul and his call to bring the Lord's name before the Gentiles (Acts 9.15).

d. The conversion of Cornelius and his family (Acts 10.1–11.18).

e. The missionary activity among Gentiles at Antioch (Acts 11.19-30).

f. The missionary tour by Barnabas and Paul (Acts 13–14) in the course of which the Jews in the synagogues tend to reject the message and the Gentiles to accept it.

4. A number of features are to be seen in these stories which indicate that *the inclusion of the Gentiles is divinely intended*:

a. The witnesses are led by various forms of divine guidance into contact with potential converts. Throughout the narrative visions of angels, guidance by prophets and direction by the Spirit are used to send the witnesses to their intended destinations.

b. There is a spontaneous reaction from the potential converts, asking for the good news to be made known to them. (Luke, of course, sees this as due to some kind of divine prompting; cf. Acts 13.48; 14.27; 16.14.) This is taken to be confirmation of the legitimacy of witnessing to them.

c. Turning to the Gentiles is associated with rejection of the message and of the witnesses by the Jews, or rather, it would appear, by a majority of them or by their leaders in any given situation. There appears to be the presumption that if the Jews reject it, the message should go to others (Acts 13.46).

d. Of especial importance is the fact that going to the Gentiles is justified by an appeal to Scripture, where the proclamation to them is seen to be prophesied (Acts 13.47).

These features have the effect of leaving the missionaries in no doubt that the proclamation to the Gentiles is an integral part of God's purpose for the spreading of the gospel.

5. However, this new move raised *problems regarding the relationships of Jews and Gentiles in the church.* These arose from the fact that the Jews regarded themselves as the special people of God by his deliberate choice of their ancestor Abraham and by the covenant made with Moses. Various features isolating them from other peoples were built into their religion—especially the observance of circumcision, worship at the temple in Jerusalem, and the keeping of the laws of Moses, particularly those regarding clean and unclean foods. The food laws had the effect of preventing the Jews from sharing food (other than that provided and cooked by themselves) with Gentiles, and constituted a major barrier to social and religious fellowship.

There was a recognized mechanism for crossing these barriers. Gentiles could gain entry to the people of God by circumcision and observance of the law. There was also a place for so-called 'God-fearers' in attendance at synagogues, although they were not regarded as belonging to the people of God.

The question which now arose for Christians was whether Gentile converts needed to undergo Jewish initiation and observe Jewish practices in order to be part of the new religious communities. It is necessary to stress that the answer to the question was by no means clear-cut. It could well have been argued that, if the new element in Christianity was simply that the messiah promised to the Jews had now arrived and the gifts of the new age were being experienced, then it was logical for new converts to accept the whole package. What grounds could there be for asserting that Gentiles could accept the messiah without all the accompaniments that were an essential part of Judaism? There was the practical argument that Jewish Christians would be religiously defiled by eating with Gentile Christians who accepted the messiah but not the Jewish way of life. And, as P.F. Esler (*Community and Gospel*, pp. 71-109) in particular has noted, it was precisely this practical consideration which stood at the fore of the debate. How, then, was it that there could be a group which insisted that Gentiles were saved and became part of God's people simply by accepting the messiah and nothing more?

As the story is related in Acts, the Ethiopian who was the first

Gentile convert simply accepted the messiah and was baptised, and no further questions were asked. The question of circumcision was not raised in Samaria because this was already a Samaritan practice; but the Samaritans were accounted unclean by the Jews all the same. The issue emerged explicitly with Cornelius, and here two points are of particular interest. First, Peter states that he had learned not to regard *anybody* as unclean (Acts 10.28)—since the abolition of the laws about clean and unclean foods implied that people were not clean or unclean in respect of what they ate. Second, the gift of the Spirit was given spontaneously to Cornelius and his family, and this qualified them for baptism. Now in the ensuing discussion in Jerusalem (Acts 11), the first point is explicitly tackled and is answered by the account of Peter's dream. The second point is dealt with by reference to the fact that the Spirit fell spontaneously upon the Gentiles, from which it could be concluded that God had given the Gentiles repentance leading to life. Consequently, there was no reason against baptising Gentiles. The implication is that the absence of circumcision did not matter.

Finally, in the account of the church at Antioch and its mission, the question of circumcising Gentile believers is not taken up at all (Acts 11.19-30).

It would seem that Luke envisages a situation in which Gentiles became Christian believers without being circumcised. We know that circumcision was not popular with non-Jews, and it may be that part of the envy shown by the Jews towards Paul's mission arose precisely because the Christian mission was more successful than the Jewish one in winning people who were not prepared to go all the way in becoming Jews. The situation may have arisen almost accidentally. But once it did arise, then the question of justifying it arose, and we have the profound argumentation in Paul's letters on the matter. It may also be the case that the 'official' Jewish rejection of Jesus raised the question whether Gentile converts needed to go through the ritual of attaching themselves to a religion which had rejected Jesus.

6. *The 'solution', as envisaged by Luke*, is found in the story of the meeting between representatives of the missionary church at Antioch and the leaders of the Jerusalem church in Acts 15. The significant features here are:

a. The demand is now explicitly for circumcision as the condition for salvation.

b. The discussion takes place against the background of a successful mission and Gentiles enjoying salvation without being circumcised.

c. The position taken by Peter is that God saves Jews and Gentiles by faith in Christ—precisely as Jews and Gentiles. That is to say, Peter does not see the church as a 'completed Judaism'. It would almost be true to say that he sees the characteristics of Judaism—circumcision and the law—as national characteristics of Jews rather than as characteristics of the people of God. Similarly, James cites Scripture to argue for God calling Gentiles to be his people—as Gentiles. Here we have a new understanding of God's purpose rather different from the 'consummation of Judaism' type of understanding. (To be sure, some would argue that James envisages one new people, with the Gentiles fulfilling certain minimal Mosaic regulations in order to be part of a consummated Judaism. However, this seems less likely.)

d. Consequently, the vital principle which emerges and which is explicitly attributed to the guidance of the Spirit is that Gentiles should not be required to be circumcised (Acts 15.28). This is regarded as 'troubling' the Gentiles and putting an 'intolerable yoke' on them.

e. However, it still makes sense for the church to avoid difficulties, and a compromise solution whereby Gentiles would not offend Jewish susceptibilities is proposed. The details are concerned with the sensitive issues of food offered in sacrifice to idols, non-'kosher' meat and sexual immorality—precisely the points which would cause greatest difficulty to orthodox Jews. (The sexual immorality referred to may be fornication, a practice against which Paul's converts needed to be warned [1 Cor. 6.12-20], or marriage between close relatives, which was forbidden by Jewish law.) This compromise is given high authority and is commended to the churches.

7. In the remainder of Acts *care for Jewish susceptibilities* is reflected in:

a. The circumcision of Timothy, whose mother was Jewish (Acts 16.3).

b. Paul's taking of a Jewish vow (Acts 18.18) and his subsequent sharing in the purification of a group of Jewish men in Jerusalem (Acts 21.23-26). All this is to demonstrate that he himself as a Jew keeps the law and does not dissuade other Jewish Christians from keeping it.

8. In the final section of Acts the position of *Christianity* (Acts 26.28!) vis-à-vis *Judaism* is discussed yet again. Paul falls foul of the secular Jewish authorities on a false charge of defiling the temple, and the rest of the story is taken up with the accusations and defence speeches arising from it. In this part of Acts the following points are noteworthy:

a. Paul's conversion is associated with Ananias, characterized as a devout Jew (Acts 22.12). His own way of life is also devout and law-abiding.

b. Yet he is called by God to be a missionary to the Gentiles.

c. He continues to quote (Acts 23.5) and obey the law. He regards himself as still faithful to his heritage as a Pharisee. The one difference in belief to which he draws attention is that he believes in the resurrection of the dead. It is clear that it is the resurrection of Jesus which is in mind (Acts 26.8, 9).

9. In the light of this summary of the evidence, we now face the question of *how Luke saw the relation between Jews, Gentiles and the church.*

a. A radical approach to the question of the church and the Jews in Acts has been followed by J.T. Sanders, who argues the case that Luke is anti-Semitic, speaking of his 'fundamental and systematic hostility' towards the Jews. Sanders' case rests on seeing a hostile attitude on the part of the Jews to the church in Acts, which leads to God's judgment upon them; this judgment is in effect shared in the attitude of the church to the Jews. The offer of the gospel is gradually withdrawn from them, and at the end of Acts the future mission is entirely directed to the Gentiles. According to Sanders, this picture is Lukan and does not correspond to the historical facts; Luke produced it in reaction to Jewish opposition to Christianity and to Jewish-Christian opposition to Gentiles in the church in his own day.

This thesis appears to confuse things that should be distinguished. It confuses the attitude of 'official' Judaism—which had condemned Jesus and which continued to attack the church—with that of individual Jews, to whom the opportunity to respond to the gospel was always open, and many of them did so according to Luke's account. Again, it is one thing to recognize that a people has come under divine judgment, and it is another to cease to love them and to withhold the gospel from them. Further, Sanders plays down the actualities of Jewish opposition to Christians and does not recognize the magnitude of it as a historical fact. He has not satisfactorily taken into account the heightened Jewish nationalism in the period leading up to the war with Rome which led to intense pressure on groups that fraternized with Gentiles. Nor does Sanders recognize adequately the concern for the Jewish people which is apparent in Luke 13.34 and 19.41-44. Luke's attitude to the Jews is much more nuanced than Sanders presents it.

b. Turning to views which see the Jews and Judaism in a more positive light, on the one side we have the view of J. Jervell (*Luke and the People of God*), who holds that for Luke there is one 'Israel', the existing people of God from which unbelieving Jews exclude themselves and to which the Gentiles can be joined by faith in Christ and by keeping those parts of the law which were binding on Gentiles. On the other side, we have the traditional view that the coming of Christ brought into existence a new people of God into which both Jews and Gentiles can enter by faith in Christ. The differences between the two views are manifestly whether there is a continuing people of God to which the Gentiles are added or a new people of God, and whether it is necessary that the law be kept not only by Jewish Christians (many of whom continue to do so, Acts 21.20-24) but also (insofar as it applies to them) by Gentile Christians.

Over against these two fairly precisely expressed positions it can of course be asked whether Luke had a consistent and self-conscious view at all. In the most thorough discussion of the issue in English, S.G. Wilson (*Gentile Mission*) holds that Luke was a pragmatist, with no carefully thought-out solution to the problem, and that his views are neither clear nor altogether consistent. Somewhat similarly, M.M.B. Turner ('Sabbath') argues that for Luke the Jerusalem Council made a breach in principle with the law and adopted a pragmatic attitude (rather than one based on principle) to the question of the observances binding on Gentiles.

c. From our discussion above it seems clear that Luke saw the Jews and the Gentiles as two distinct groups from which God was trying to bring people to faith in Jesus, and specifically he was creating 'a people for his name' from the Gentiles. This strongly supports the view that Luke is interested in the gathering of a people who believe in Jesus; if they are Jews, they may retain their ancestral customs—but they must enter into fellowship with uncircumcised Gentile believers; if they are Gentiles, they do not need to become Jews, but they should take steps to avoid antagonizing Jewish believers. It is significant that the motivation for observance of the law by Gentile Christians is in order to avoid causing offence to Jews (Acts 15.21?; 16.3; 21.20-25). That is to say, the observance of parts of the law by Gentiles is not a matter of principle but of expediency. And in the case of the Jews, although Paul and others are presented as faithful to the law (Acts 21.20-24; 24.14; 25.8), the abolition of the clean–unclean foods distinction indicates that the path to a new way of life was opening up. (It is a moot point whether Paul in reality was as observant of the Jewish law as Acts makes out. It is often argued that the non-mention of the Jerusalem 'agreement' in 1 Corinthians 8–10 suggests that he did not know of it or did not approve of it and that he took a firmer line on Gentile freedom from the law. See further the discussion in my commentary [1980], pp. 242-47, 260-61.)

At the same time, faith in Jesus is seen as the consummation of Judaism in that the coming of the messiah, Jesus, is the hope of Israel, and the coming of the messiah and the establishment of the church are all part of a divine plan, adumbrated in the prophetic Scriptures.

The Common Life of the Witnesses

A major omission in Acts is any detailed account of the life of the church. Luke does have a theology of the church as the people of God, the flock which he bought with the blood of his own Son (Acts 20.28) and which is composed of people who have passed out of darkness into light, and out of the realm of Satan into the kingdom of God (Acts 26.18). He describes to some extent the nature and activity of the first group of disciples in Jerusalem, and he even spends time on events that do not appear to be germane to his main purpose (the Ananias and Sapphira episode); he also gives some account of the nature of the life of the church at Antioch, but for the rest he is describing the work of missionaries who in the nature of things were present at the foundation of churches and then moved on elsewhere. Although, then, Acts could be regarded as presenting a paradigm for the mission of the church, it does not in any way present a detailed paradigm for the ongoing life of the church. It follows that for the most part we learn about the life of the church through incidental remarks rather than through deliberate, extended discussion and description. What, then, does Luke reveal about the life of the church and its internal needs?

1. Right from the beginning the church is *a group which assembles*

together. For the most part the 'piety' in Acts is a group activity.
Individual Christians (and Jews) may pray on their own (Peter,
Cornelius, Paul immediately after his conversion), but in general
Luke describes Christians as meeting together for common activities.
Initial entry into membership of the group is by the rite of baptism
with water, with which the laying on of hands is sometimes associated.

2. A frequent feature of these assemblies is *prayer* (Acts 1.14; 2.42;
4.24-31; 12.12). Prayer also precedes important decisions (Acts 1.24-
25; 6.6). Its content is mainly petition and preparation for the activity
of God. Joy, praise and thanksgiving to God are likewise characteristic of the Christian meetings (Acts 2.46-47).

3. *Teaching* of various kinds is also important. An evening meeting
could contain an address given by Paul of such length that one of the
hearers fell into a deep sleep (Acts 20.7-11). The activity of prophets
is mentioned, and it appears to have consisted in bringing specific
directions from God in particular situations, as well as exhorting and
encouraging people in a more general way. Alongside prophets we
also hear of the teaching of the apostles and others. The distinction
between prophetic and non-prophetic activity is hard to define; it
presumably has something to do with a person feeling directly
inspired by God to convey a certain message rather than excogitating
a message by his own efforts.

4. The disciples meet together to '*break bread*' (i.e. celebrate the
Lord's Supper, in Paul's terminology) and to eat meals together. This
is mentioned at the outset, and then later only in 20.7, where it is
referred to as a normal occurrence on the first day of the week, and
possibly in 27.33-38. Luke does not describe it in any detail.

5. The activity of *women* in the church is again something that is
mentioned in passing. The significant items are that a church can be
begun simply with a group of women (Acts 16.13), and that a woman
(named before her husband!) shares in Paul's missionary work and
specifically in instructing another missionary whose Christian knowledge is defective (Acts 18.26).

6. Acts does not display a lot of interest in the details of *leadership*
of the church. The task of witness is assigned by divine command to
the Twelve at the outset. They appear to function as leaders in virtue
of their qualifications as witnesses, but at some point (on which Luke
is tantalizingly vague) Peter and the rest of the Twelve give way to a
leadership group of James and the elders, which is presumably

modelled on existing Jewish patterns of synagogue leadership. The apostles, in consultation with the church, appoint the Seven to share in leadership roles at Jerusalem, and the missionaries appoint 'elders' in the churches which they found (Acts 14.22). Paul himself chooses those who share in his work—and rejects some possible candidates. Other people are called to specific tasks by direct divine command.

Social Problems in the Community

One of the features of Luke–Acts which has aroused intense interest in recent study, doubtless because of contemporary concern with the issue of *Rich Christians in an Age of Hunger* (to use the title of Ronald J. Sider's influential book), is its teaching, direct and implied, about the question of wealth and poverty. Interest has centred principally upon the Gospel, where it is clear that Luke's interest in this theme has led him to give greater place to it than the other Gospels. But the theme is also present in Acts, although to a lesser extent. Luke envisages a church whose members are drawn from different strata of society. This would be only natural if any wealthy people with households were converted, since the likelihood is that the household or 'family' would share the conversion of the head of the household. In the earliest days in Jerusalem, some kind of communal sharing of possessions was practised for the benefit of those who were needy (Acts 2.44-45; 4.32, 34-6; 6.1-6), and dishonesty in regard to this was treated with the utmost seriousness (Acts 5.1-11). But apart from this Acts has little to say on the theme.

From a historical point of view, it would not be surprising if some kind of sharing was practised in a tightly-knit group; something similar is attested for the Qumran sect, and their rites of initiation, which included the handing over of private property for the benefit of the community, have been used to illuminate the early Christian practice (B.J. Capper, 'Interpretation of Acts 5.4'). The difficulty with this suggestion is that it requires that there was a period of probation before full membership, for which we have no evidence in the early church.

There is no mention of the practice at Jerusalem being extended elsewhere, and the way in which other churches made monetary contributions to help the Christians in Jerusalem from time to time may suggest that it was not continued there or even that it was unsuccessful.

Acts mentions financial aid from Antioch to Jerusalem (Acts 11.27-30), and there is a surprisingly casual reference to the gifts Paul brought to Jerusalem in Acts 24.17. The explanation for the comparative lack of interest in the topic after the early chapters may be threefold. First, Luke appears to assume that the readers of Acts will 'take as read' what has already been said in the Gospel (compare his silence in Acts on the judgment against Jerusalem). Secondly, Luke often mentions something once and expects his readers to extrapolate it to other situations. And, thirdly, since Luke is interested basically in the evangelistic witness of the church, he does not go into details of the common life of the different congregations. From what Paul says in Acts 20.33-35 we can see that the tradition of freedom from covetousness and sharing one's possessions with others continued as an ideal to be practised. That this is not a Lukan invention or a piece of idealism is abundantly evident from Paul's teaching in his letters (2 Cor. 8–9).

Christians and the State Authorities

Like the question of riches and poverty, the attitude of Christians to the secular world has become a centre of contemporary interest in NT study. We have already discussed theories which suggest that Luke's purpose, or one of his purposes, in writing was to present an apologia for Christians over against accusations from outside the church, and that such apologetic is focused on the case of Paul in his conflicts with both the Jewish leaders and the Roman administration. This type of theory has been questioned by R.J. Cassidy (*Society and Politics*), who dismisses the view that Luke was writing any form of apologetic, and argues instead that Luke wrote to strengthen the allegiance to Christ of his readers, to guide them on how to live as disciples in the context of Roman rule, and specifically to give them perspective and guidance, should they stand on trial before political officials.

The possibility of hostility from the outside world was very real to the early church. Even today the occurrence of an isolated terrorist attack can rouse an exaggerated fear of widespread outbursts (compare the way in which air passenger traffic dropped dramatically even on domestic flights within North America during the Gulf War thousands of miles away). The same was true in the ancient world. That this question was present to Luke's mind is shown by Luke 12.11-12 and

21.12-15, where the disciples are told that they will face such trials and that the Holy Spirit will give them the right words to say. Acts shows this very thing happening. But, although they are to rely on the Spirit, Luke still envisages the need for Christians themselves to take care to act in the right way. There is plenty of appropriate material in Acts; hostility and confrontation with the Jewish leaders, with mobs and with state authorities are to be found in something like twenty separate incidents in Acts. Witness undoubtedly takes place in a hostile environment. The picture of non-retaliation and even prayer for opponents is surely meant as a pattern to be followed.

Yet, despite Cassidy's claims, it is surely the case that Acts does deliberately contain material which emphasizes that the lives of Christians are, or should be, free from conduct which would be a legitimate cause for action by the Roman state. The accusations brought against them are unjust.

Admittedly, Luke shows that the Christian way of life brings its practitioners into conflict with people who do not share it. Where the leaders of another religion or the rulers of the state forbid Christian witness, the church must stand firm against their requirements and insist on its freedom to obey God rather than earthly authorities, and it recognizes that such loyalty to Christ will be costly.

P.F. Esler (*Community and Gospel*, pp. 201-219) argues that Luke was influenced by the presence of Romans in the church who had a continuing allegiance to their state, perhaps because they served it in military or political positions. In his view, Luke's concern is to legitimate Christianity in the eyes of Roman Christians who had to face the fact that it was the Roman power which had executed Jesus and attacked his followers. He therefore shows that Christians had done nothing which would bring them into conflict with Roman laws, and that, where they were attacked, it was a case of injustice by individual Roman officials. Rome had respect for the ancestral religions of its subject peoples, and therefore Luke stresses the historical roots of Christianity in Judaism.

The merit of this hypothesis is that it suggests a much more plausible audience for Acts than the outside world. If there were Christian Roman officials in the church, they would be a part of the audience who would read what Luke wrote. The difficulty with the proposal is that there is no independent evidence that there were Roman Christians who were conscious of this as a problem, and therefore it remains an inference from the text of Acts.

From this survey of some of the topics relating to the life of the church in Acts we see that Luke paints a picture which needs to be brought into relationship with what we can learn from elsewhere in the NT about the way in which things actually developed, and the question arises whether Luke has given a faithful impression of what happened or has given us an idealistic, even a tendentious picture.

Further Reading

B.J. Capper, 'The Interpretation of Acts 5.4', *JSNT* 19 (1983), pp. 117-31.

R.J. Cassidy, *Society and Politics in the Acts of the Apostles* (Maryknoll: Orbis Books, 1987).

P.J. Esler, *Community and Gospel in Luke–Acts* (Cambridge: Cambridge University Press, 1987).

J. Jervell, *Luke and the People of God* (Minneapolis: Augsburg, 1972).

M.M.B. Turner, 'Jesus and the Spirit in Lucan Perspective', *TynBul* 32 (1981), pp. 3-42.

—'The Sabbath, Sunday and the Law in Luke–Acts', in D.A. Carson (ed.), *From Sabbath to Lord's Day: A Biblical, Historical and Theological Investigation* (Grand Rapids: Zondervan, 1982), pp. 99-157.

J.T. Sanders, *The Jews in Luke–Acts* (London: SCM Press, 1987).

H. Strathmann, 'μάρτυς, κτλ', in *TDNT*, IV, pp. 474-514.

R. Stronstad, *The Charismatic Theology of St Luke* (Peabody, MA: Hendrickson, 1984).

S.G. Wilson, *The Gentiles and the Gentile Mission in Luke–Acts* (Cambridge: Cambridge University Press, 1973).

—*Luke and the Law* (Cambridge: Cambridge University Press, 1983).

5

HISTORY AND
THEOLOGY IN ACTS

SO FAR WE HAVE BEEN looking mainly at what Luke has to say in Acts, considered as a theological message to the church of his time. In so doing he has given us a representation of the early history and theology of the church. The question that must eventually be addressed concerns the kind of relationship that Luke's record bears to what actually happened. To what extent is the *picture* of what the early church did, believed and proclaimed historically reliable?

The historical value of Acts has had a hard time in recent years. Much of biblical study operates on the basis of a 'hermeneutics of suspicion' which critically examines what an author says to see if it is acceptable, whether as a factual narrative or as morally and spiritually valid. The trouble with such an approach is that it tends to be biased towards discovering problems. At the same time, the approach which assumes that a narrative is historically reliable until it is proved beyond doubt to be otherwise can be equally uncritical and lacking in sane judgment. Somehow an approach must be attempted which is free from doctrinaire suspicion or credulousness.

However, for many scholars today this issue appears to be unimportant. They have passed beyond the stage of discussing historical questions at all, and they would argue that study of a text as a literary composition can and should be carried on regardless of any historical questions that may arise. But if I am right in claiming that Luke intended to write history, then his competence as a historian is a valid and necessary subject for investigation. This issue is manifestly important for Christian readers who claim that their religion has its basis in a series of historical events in which they see the actions and the revelation of God. Is their claim justified? Clearly, the question whether the events are to be interpreted as acts in which God is active lies beyond the scope of the historian, but the question as to whether the events happened at all, or in the way in which they are related, is a matter for the historian. There is a legitimate and necessary 'quest for the historical early church', just as there is for 'the historical Jesus'. We must therefore survey contemporary discussion of this problem.

The History of Criticism

In the nineteenth century the view which increasingly came to prevail (under the influence of the Tübingen School) was that the picture painted in Acts was highly unreliable. F.C. Baur started from what he saw as significant difficulties in the text: (a) the accounts of miraculous events which could not be taken as sober history; and (b) the absence from Acts of the conflict between Peter and Paul which is attested in Galatians. He concluded that the author of Acts was painting a tendentious and hence inaccurate picture of Christian origins in the interests of commending a so-called 'early catholicism' which smoothed over the actual conflicts in the church between the factions of Peter and Paul. The result was a classical example of the detection of a Hegelian pattern in history: the strongly Jewish, legalistic Christianity of Peter (the *thesis*) generated its polar opposite, the strongly Gentile, law-free Christianity of Paul (the *antithesis*), and these in turn gave way to the compromise, the harmonizing form of early catholicism (the *synthesis*). Luke's work represented the presentation of early Christianity in a manner which smoothed out the early, bitter history and allowed early catholicism to claim to represent truly the original nature of Christianity.

Round the turn of the century a reaction set in with the work of such scholars as W.M. Ramsay, F.H. Chase and A. Wikenhauser who attempted to demonstrate that Acts was not written as late as Baur and his school had supposed and (especially in the case of Ramsay) to accumulate archaeological evidence which confirmed that Acts was faithfully reflecting the geographical, social and political conditions of the middle part of the first century. Ramsay, indeed, was led to praise Luke as being outstanding among ancient historians for his reliability; granted that he expressed himself somewhat extravagantly, this is still a testimony that ought not to be lightly dismissed (W.M. Ramsay, *Recent Discovery*, pp. 80-81, 222).

Critical response was inevitable, particularly against some of the more extreme expressions of this general position—e.g. that the use of medical language in Luke–Acts proved that the author was a medical doctor. The centre of attention initially was the speech material in Acts; here H.J. Cadbury and M. Dibelius argued strongly that this reflected the theological interests of Luke rather than any actual sermons by the apostles. Dibelius and others, especially E. Haenchen, went on to apply form-criticism and redaction-criticism to Acts, and they showed that a considerable amount of material could be understood as due either to changes brought about in the course of the tradition-process or to the editorial work of Luke himself. Haenchen argued that Luke had few, if any, recognizable sources, and that a very great deal of the narrative could be fully explained as originating in his own mind. The first question to be asked was not 'What happened?', but 'What was Luke trying to do?', and once that question had been answered, there was not much need to ask any further questions. Luke's motives could adequately explain the shaping, and often the genesis, of much in the book. Haenchen in particular showed the fruitfulness of continually asking what Luke himself was trying to do in any given pericope; his rigorous historical scepticism and his belief that written sources could scarcely be detected behind the narrative strengthened his view that, although Luke was a historian, he enjoyed a freedom which we today would allow only to a historical novelist.

Haenchen's view was very influential, expressed by him as it was in the major critical commentary on Acts to appear in this period. It was also backed up by the work of H. Conzelmann, whose own commentary on Acts could do little more than echo the views of his predecessor. Replies from the more traditional side were largely lacking. The major work of F.F. Bruce, while fully aware of Dibelius and his challenge to conservative views, did not engage too directly with it and of course preceded Haenchen. Only R.P.C. Hanson took account of Haenchen and showed up some of his weaknesses.

This consensus has been challenged once again by renewed claims that Luke's work is to be seen as based on material of historical worth. Three scholars call for mention here.

M. Hengel

In his comparatively brief discussion M. Hengel is concerned to mediate between the two extreme positions which he sees in the field at present. His complaint is that scholarship has tended to polarize between a non-critical approach, which does not raise critical questions about historicity, and a radical sceptical approach, which tends to question whether any historical basis can be determined behind the text. On the one hand, there is the type of approach which avoids asking historical questions and assumes that the text, as it stands, can be taken as historically reliable. On the other, there is the approach which insists that the text is so far removed from the original events by (a) the passage of time, (b) the changes introduced in the tradition-process and (c) the redactional creativity of the author, that the historical question has become unanswerable in principle; the end-result is an agnosticism, which in practice means historical scepticism. Both views are unjustified.

As regards the former approach, we may observe that even the most conservative student of the New Testament who holds on theological grounds that it is the Word of God—and therefore true—must nevertheless deal with problems such as why the details of the story of Paul's conversion vary from one account to another, or why there is a discrepancy between material in Acts and reports of the same incident in Josephus. Such a student may produce a harmonizing explanation, but even such an explanation is a piece of historical and critical study, and the decisive questions will be whether a given solution commends itself as reasonable in itself over against other possibilities, and whether it is probable, given what we know of the general tendency of the author as regards historical accuracy or inaccuracy. It is necessary to determine in what sense Acts is a reliable account, and how far its reliability or otherwise is related to the presentation of one-sided or incomplete narratives.

Equally, the radical position is untenable. It decides not to ask the historical question because it is believed that there is neither enough information nor sufficiently refined methods to make it capable of being answered. But abandonment of the historical quest on the ground that the accounts are so tendentious and legendary that no critical methods can successfully analyse them for a historical basis is unjustified. There is sufficient material in Acts which can be corroborated from other, independent sources to demonstrate that historical incidents do lie behind it, and it is possible to develop methods of analysis which help us to cope with them.

Hengel regards Acts as a kind of historical monograph and states quite categorically that 'Luke is no less trustworthy than other historians of antiquity' (*Acts and the History*, p. 60)—a remark which must be taken in the context of Hengel's comments on the faults of which ancient historians were capable. He argues that Luke did not make it his purpose to set out his own theology but rather to go back to the beginnings in an attempt to record the events that constituted the foundation for faith. On this basis he attempts a reconstruction of the earliest history of the church from the events recorded in Acts 6 to Acts 15.

Hengel's observations are interesting and important, but it is a pity that he did not take the space to justify more fully what might appear to be rather dogmatic statements. We have to turn to other scholars for the detailed outworking of the approach which he advocates.

G. Lüdemann

The task has been taken up systematically by G. Lüdemann in what amounts to a historical commentary on Acts. He reacts against the bracketing off of the historical question by the dominant school of scholarship in Acts, and he offers a method which has two parts to it. First, it is necessary to distinguish between tradition and redaction in Acts, using the tools of stylistic and theological analysis to identify what originates with Luke himself. Here Lüdemann is working on the assumptions (a) that Luke has made use of traditional material, and (b) that his own redaction of it has no historical value (or at least cannot be assumed to have such). Then, second, the traditional material is subjected to historical analysis in order to determine what may reasonably be regarded as historical in the light of other evidence and general probability. Lüdemann's approach is not without its problems.

First, he assumes rather too easily that whatever can be identified as redactional can be ignored for the purposes of historical reconstruction. Clearly a proper attitude of caution is warranted, but Lüdemann ignores the three possibilities: (a) that Luke had access to historical information which he inserted at the redactional stage; (b) that Luke's redactional concerns and the tradition could at times coincide (e.g. Luke and Peter may have shared some theological expressions or concepts); and (c) that material expressed in Lukan style may be simply tradition put in his own words or manner of expression rather than his own creation.

Secondly, once Lüdemann has peeled away the redaction from the tradition, his analysis of its historicity appears at times to be arbitrary and impressionistically based. It raises the general question of how one determines historicity.

Thirdly, Lüdemann holds a theory of the chronology of the church which requires that Luke has seriously misunderstood the situation, and this alleged flaw in Luke's knowledge of Paul leads him to adopt a sceptical attitude to the narrative in general. However, this chronology in fact is far from convincing and is certainly not proved. Despite Lüdemann's own sanguine claims (*Paul, Apostle to the Gentiles*, pp. 289-94) regarding reaction to his chronology, it has been strongly criticized. It is a very dubious basis for far-reaching theories about the credibility of Luke. Nevertheless, it remains true that Lüdemann is far more positive about the historical value of Acts than has recently been fashionable.

C.J. Hemer

A very different approach is taken by C.J. Hemer, who stands more in the succession of Ramsay. In a monumental work he has gone over the archaeological material once again and produced much fresh evidence to show that Acts reflects the life of the middle of the first century and that its background details receive considerable corroboration from secular sources. Hemer concludes that Luke is much more reliable historically than he is often given credit for.

Hemer's general approach is open to question at a number of points.

1. First, there is the question of whether the background details are as reliable as is asserted. Hemer is clearly tempted to ascribe a very high standard of accuracy to Luke. Thus he writes about the historical problem created by the mention of Theudas before Judas in Acts 5.36-37:

> Yet even if Luke has committed an anachronism by placing these words on Gamaliel's lips and has reversed the order of the two uprisings, one such slip on his part would not entitle us to argue for his general unreliability. The fact that Luke's background information can so often be

corroborated may suggest that it is wiser to leave this particular matter open rather than to condemn Luke of a blunder (*Acts in the Setting of Hellenistic History*, p. 163).

There is, however, the danger that critics who feel that Hemer has gone too far in his second sentence here may tend to ignore the perfectly valid point made in the first sentence, namely that even the most reliable of historians may still make a number of errors of fact and errors in judgment. Further, it must be observed that Hemer has cast his net fairly widely, and there are few aspects of the Graeco-Roman background in Acts which he does not investigate. (One can hardly fault him for not discussing the census of Quirinius which falls outside his immediate remit.)

2. Secondly, there is the fundamental methodological question as to whether one can argue on the basis of accuracy in background detail for accuracy of main plot. Modern novelists may research a story in considerable detail to provide an accurate background for fictitious events (witness the work of F. Forsyth). But in this case we are dealing with a definable type of modern writer who writes what is freely admitted to be fiction with an appearance of authenticity and verisimilitude. No deception is involved; there may even be a disclaimer at the beginning! But this does not look at all like what Luke is doing. Luke–Acts purports to be a truthful record and not something which is professedly a novel—which would not have been appropriate in the ecclesiastical setting. And what conceivable motives could Luke have had for writing deliberate fiction? Nor is there any indication of careful background research by Luke into areas with which he was not personally familiar. The impression is rather of an author who is at home in the period which he describes, and of course the closer he is to that period, the less likely it is that he would be writing a fictitious account that was out of touch with reality.

Putting the matter in this way shows that two related questions are involved. First, there is the question of what Luke was intending to do. The case is that he was attempting to write a historical record of some kind. Secondly, there is the question of what he actually did. If he was writing a historical record, the presumption is that he attempted to get the story right. However, it by no means follows that he necessarily did so all the way through. We can easily think of reasons why he may not have produced this result.

1. He may have received mistaken information from his informants and nor been in a position to check it and correct it.
2. He may not have had full information and found it necessary to use some imagination in describing what probably took place.
3. He may have been affected by unconscious bias which led him to overlook certain things or to present material from a tendentious angle.
4. He may have had conscious motives for telling the story in a particular manner, whether by being economical with the truth, or by introducing bias.

Any of these things could happen even with a careful writer. In the case of Luke it is to be admitted that he was not simply a historian, giving an annalistic account of events, but that he was a theologian and pastor writing for the benefit of the church. The history was there to serve a purpose. But if so, has the theological outlook affected the telling of the story? Has Hemer ignored Lukan theology and its possible impact on the composition?

But this common assumption that theological concern necessarily implies an indifference to history and even a readiness to reconstruct history is extremely dubious; the fact of historical precision in areas that can be tested strongly suggests that there are limits to the way in which theological concern can shape narratives which purport to be historical, and that a concern for history and a concern for theology can be mutually compatible rather than irreconcilable.

What Hemer is doing is to ask about Luke's performance where it can be checked. If what is in effect a somewhat arbitrary probe reveals a reasonable level of authorial care and accuracy, then it is legitimate to proceed with due caution from the sample to the whole.

To some readers it may well seem to be the case that Hemer claims too much for Luke. Nevertheless, even if he does go too far, it would be wrong to claim that his case is lacking in substance and to attempt to dismiss it to the sidelines of modern study. On the contrary, his work in combination with that of Hengel and Lüdemann shows that the Haenchen–Conzelmann consensus can no longer be accepted without question as the basis for future study of Acts. There is a case that Acts gives a truer picture of what actually happened than Haenchen or Pervo would allow, although this is not to say that Luke has given us a blow-by-blow account of every detail in the story or that he has not given it some literary and theological shaping.

The Career of Paul in Acts

One particular area affords the possibility of comparison and a verdict. This is the career and theology of Paul as it is reported in Acts and in his own letters. It is not surprising that this has come to be at the centre of the discussion as a test case. What are we to make of it?

In earlier studies it was customary to reconstruct the career of Paul by using the story in Acts as a framework into which to place the letters at appropriate points. Nowadays it is considered methodologically more appropriate to use the primary evidence (i.e. those letters generally considered to be authentic) as the basis and then fit in the evidence from Acts. Yet, as Hengel says:

> Without the account written by Luke, incomplete, fragmentary and misleading though it may be, we would not only find it almost impossible to put Paul and his work in a chronological and geographical setting; we would still be largely in the dark about the development of Paul's great mission around the Aegean and the events that led up to it (*Acts and the History*, p. 38).

The biggest problems that emerge concern (1) the nature of Paul's conversion; (2) the relationship of Paul to Jerusalem and his self-understanding; (3) the chronology of the missionary journeys; (4) the history of the Jew–Gentile problem and, in particular, the relation between Paul's discussion with the church leaders in Jerusalem in Galatians 2 and the visits recorded in Acts; (5) the collection for Jerusalem; (6) Paul's theology. Let us consider these in turn.

1. *Paul's Conversion*
The event commonly called 'Paul's conversion' is described briefly by Paul himself in Galatians 1, and there are three detailed accounts of it in Acts 9, 22 and 26. Some scholars have suggested that there are problems in the fact that sometimes the event has more the character of a conversion experience and in others more that of a calling to mission. Thus G. Lüdemann (*Early Christianity*, pp. 115-116) has argued that the event has more the character of a conversion in Acts 9 and of a missionary call in Acts 22 and 26 as well as in Galatians. This leads to the suggestion that it is Luke who has turned the story into

one of a conversion in Acts 9 and underemphasized the 'call' elements which surface in Acts 22 and 26.

However, this analysis is mistaken. Already in Acts 9 Luke is preparing the way for the mission to the Gentiles, and Acts 9.15 clearly incorporates this point (*pace* Lüdemann). Further, the alleged distinction between a conversion and a missionary calling is false. The missionary calling must presuppose a conversion, and the combination of the two events in one is perfectly natural; conversion is implicit in Galatians 1.

G. Lohfink (*The Conversion of St Paul*) argues that Paul's silence about the incident in his letters makes it unlikely that he would have told the story to anybody in detail. But, while it is true that in 2 Cor. 12.1-4 Paul is reserved about his own spiritual experiences, this is in relation to the 'false apostles' who stressed signs and wonders rather than in relation to personal witness. There is some difference between telling one's conversion story ostentatiously to an audience in public and speaking about it in a more restrained way in a smaller company of colleagues and friends.

Clearly there is much more detail in the accounts in Acts. Yet there is nothing in Acts which contradicts the summary in Galatians. The basic fact in all the accounts is that Paul saw Jesus and came to recognize him as the Son of God.

2. *Paul's Self-Understanding and the Church in Jerusalem*
Closely connected with the conversion/calling of Paul is his relationship to the church in Jerusalem and his role in relation to that of the original apostles. Lohfink argues that Luke fudges the issue of the nature of Paul's experience in order to avoid the implication that it was like that of the original apostles. But he has to admit that according to Luke Paul did see Jesus in a christophany, just as he himself claims in his letters. Paul had no doubts that his experience was comparable to that of the original apostles. The differences in presentation in Luke's account are surely due solely to the fact that Paul's experience was historically later than those of the original apostles and took place in the different situation after the ascension.

Lohfink also argues that Luke's Paul sees himself as different from the original apostles who are 'the witnesses to the people' (Acts 13.31-33). Linked with this is the fact that Luke refers to Paul as an apostle only in Acts 14.4, 14, despite the fact that for Paul his apostleship is the principal item in his self-identity in the church. There is, of course, no disputing that Luke sees a special role for the Twelve who had been companions of Jesus as well as witnesses to his resurrection, and Paul did not share the first of these two qualifications. Luke reserves the name of 'apostle' for the Twelve apart from in Acts 14. However, it must be stressed that the function of being 'witnesses' is the principal one in Acts, and both the Twelve and Paul come together under this umbrella term. Luke does not deny Paul's apostleship, but equally he confines the term to the role of the Twelve in relation to the people of Israel in line with the choice of Jesus in the Gospels (see especially Lk. 22.28-30).

In conjunction with this Lohfink also argues that Luke saw Paul's calling as being mediated through the church by means of Ananias. Acts 26.16-18, where Luke ascribes Paul's call directly to the Lord, speaks clearly against this suggestion; for Luke, Ananias is the spokesman of the Lord, not of the church. Here the wider question of the events directly after Paul's conversion also arises. In Galatians he is fiercely independent of the church at Jerusalem and emphasizes that it was only three years after his conversion that he went to Jerusalem and even then stayed for only a short time and saw few people. In Acts 9, however, his first visit to Jerusalem appears to come shortly after his conversion and he spends some time there witnessing among the Hellenists. It may readily be granted that Luke has created a difficulty by not mentioning the time Paul spent in Arabia. But the main difficulty raised by critics appears to arise from the assumption that Luke makes Paul subject to Jerusalem; this in turn leads to finding a significance in the narrative that was never intended. Acts 9.27 refers to *recognition* of Paul by the apostles in Jerusalem; it hardly suggests *subjection* to them.

3. *The Chronology of the Missionary Journeys*
The missionary activity of Paul in Acts is divided up into three missionary 'journeys' (Acts 13-14; 15.36-18.17; 18.18-20.38) with the Jerusalem 'council' coming between the first and the second of these. It has been argued that this presentation is purely schematic, and the placing of the council has been much debated. The chronology of Paul's journeys remains a complicated problem. Mention has been made previously of Lüdemann's drastic reconstruction (*Paul, Apostle to the Gentiles*) which in effect puts the first and second journeys

before the Council. Three points deserve attention here.

First, the presentation in Acts does note that Paul spent considerable periods of time in certain major centres (Corinth, Ephesus) and would have spent longer in others had he not been forced to leave (Thessalonica, Philippi). The picture of the touring missionary making whistle-stop halts in many places is a false impression. We should speak of missionary 'campaigns' rather than 'journeys'. A carefully organized and planned operation was being undertaken. This is in agreement with Paul's own picture of his work in Romans 15.

Secondly, in Galatians Paul's mission to the Gentiles is acknowledged and recognized by the Jerusalem church. In his letters he displays some kind of connection with that church and takes a collection from the Gentile churches to it. The picture in Acts is interesting. The first missionary tour is done under the aegis of the church at Antioch to which Paul and Barnabas are in effect responsible. Thereafter, Paul acts more on his own initiative (Acts 15.36). He visits Jerusalem in between his second and third tours (Acts 18.22), but Luke mentions this so briefly and casually that any question of Paul being subservient to the church simply does not arise.

Thirdly, what Luke says about Paul's missionary practice, especially his going to regions not previously evangelized and his work with a team of colleagues and helpers, fits in well with what Paul says in his letters and significantly fills out the picture in various aspects.

4. *The Jew–Gentile Problem and the Jerusalem Council*

The major historical question in Acts is constituted by the events associated with the meeting described in Acts 15. There is a strong consensus that the account of Paul's meeting with the Jerusalem leaders in Galatians 2.1-10 is basically accurate, and that the account in Acts 15 is in considerable contradiction to it, especially in the fact that the council issues a directive concerning conditions to be imposed on Gentile converts which Paul accepts and is prepared to disseminate in the churches. It is argued that to have done so would have been a compromise that went against Paul's principles. Hence the account in Acts is regarded as being partly based on what did transpire at the council and partly as being based on another meeting (not attended by Paul). Further, the question as to when the council met in relation to other events is debatable; some scholars would equate it with the visit by Paul in Acts 18.22 and/or deny the historicity of the visit in Acts 11.30.

An alternative scenario is that there were two meetings to discuss the same basic issue, the place of the Gentiles in the church, one of a more informal and private nature at the time of Paul's visit in Acts 11.30, which is described in Galatians 2, and the other of a more formal character at the time of Paul's visit to Jerusalem in Acts 15. At the latter meeting the freedom of the Gentiles from circumcision was fully agreed, but certain rulings to ease the problem of table fellowship in the church were agreed.

The topic and indeed the whole question of the history of Jew–Gentile relationships in the early church is too complex to be discussed in detail here. Both of the positions outlined have their difficulties, but the detailed discussion by R.N. Longenecker (*Galatians*) demonstrates that a very strong case can be made for the second scenario. If this is correct, a major objection to Luke's historical reliability at this point would be removed.

5. *The Collection for Jerusalem*
It has often been thought strange that whereas in some of his major letters Paul attaches great importance to the collection of a sum of money from the Gentile churches for the church in Jerusalem and his journey to Jerusalem to deliver it, in Acts what is to be identified as this visit proceeds without any direct mention of it. The most that is said is that Paul came 'to bring alms to my nation and to offer sacrifices' (Acts 24.17). This curious description is amply explained by the fact that Paul is here on trial before Felix on charges preferred by the Jewish authorities, and therefore he uses language that will put the best possible construction on his action. Yet this is the *only* reference in Acts to the collection, and it is purely incidental, passing almost without notice. The solution offered by F.F. Bruce and G. Lüdemann (among others) is that Luke (or his source) knew that the collection did not have the desired effect of helping good relations between the Jerusalem church and the Gentile churches, and therefore he quietly passed over it. It may indeed well be that the situation in Jerusalem was such that no amount of gifts from the churches could silence the complaints that the bringer of the gifts was alleged to be dissuading Jewish believers from circumcision and the customs required by the law. Paul feared profoundly what kind of reception he might get in

Jerusalem both from the Jews in general and even from the church
(Rom. 15.30-31). It is not surprising that he did his best to persuade
people of his essential Jewishness when he arrived, and that the
collection failed to accomplish its purpose.

6. Paul's theology

There remains the problem of Luke's presentation of Paul's theology
in Acts. In fact there is not a lot of it, since what Luke gives us are
basically Paul's missionary sermons, his brief pastoral address to the
church leaders gathered at Miletus, and his speeches in his own
defence when on trial. Much of the kind of material which is found in
the letters—in particular Paul's discussion of the doctrine and practice
of the Christian life—is lacking because it lies outside the purpose of
the author. At the same time, the kind of material which is found in
Acts is not found in the letters to any great extent. The missionary
preaching of Paul can be reconstructed only indirectly, since the
letters are written to converts. Nevertheless, a basic similarity between
the speeches to Gentiles and the preaching, as reconstructed from
passages like 1 Thess. 1.9-10, can be observed. Paul's defence in Acts
is basically against Jewish attacks, whereas in the letters he is dealing
with rivalry and opposition within the church.

Despite the fact, then, that Acts and the letters contain mostly material that is not directly comparable, the question remains as to whether
what emerges about the underlying theology of Paul is in harmony
between the two sources. Scholarship has not really gone much further since P. Vielhauer's influential essay, 'The "Paulinism" of Acts'
(in Keck and Martyn [eds.], *Studies in Luke–Acts*, pp. 33-50), in
which he argued that Luke got it wrong with respect to Paul's attitude
to natural theology, to the law, to Christology and to eschatology—a
fairly comprehensive list!

a. So far as natural theology, or better 'creation theology', is concerned, a contrast has been drawn between what Paul says in Athens in
Acts 17 and to the Romans in Romans 1.18-19. In the former he uses
his audience's religious beliefs as a point of contact in evangelism,
while in the latter he reflects that though people have a knowledge of
God from his acts in creation they have not followed it through but
have turned to idolatry. What Paul says in Acts 17 (and in Acts 14) is
paralleled in 1 Thess. 1.9-10, and F.F. Bruce has rightly commented
that if you take the person who wrote Romans 1 and put him down in

Athens he will probably say the kind of things that Luke reports. In short, the different audiences and purposes of the two allegedly contradictory passages have not been taken into account by critics.

b. Paul's personal attitude to observance of the law in Acts is the same as in his letters. The circumcision of Timothy (Acts 16.3) was because of his Jewish parentage on his mother's side, and was in no way contrary to Paul's principles. Again, the problem is one of complementarity. In his letters Paul is defending the freedom of the Gentiles from the law, whereas in Acts Luke is demonstrating the complementary fact that Paul was not opposed to Jewish Christians continuing in their Jewish way of life. To be sure, Luke does not reveal the intense struggles that Paul personally had over the whole problem, but this was not part of his purpose.

c. The lack of reference to the pre-existence of Christ and to the saving character of his death in Acts has been discussed above (see Chapter 3).

d. It is suggested that Paul believes intensely in the imminent parousia of Christ, whereas this belief has been significantly weakened in Acts; Luke no longer believes in the contemporaneity of the 'already' and the 'not yet' of the new age, but has placed them in a temporal dualism. This evaluation, however, rests on a mistaken assumption regarding how imminent early Christians believed the parousia to be—Paul certainly thought that the conditions for the coming of the end of the world were not yet fulfilled (Rom. 11), and he shared Luke's conception of God's ongoing plan of salvation-history. Luke for his part certainly believed that the end-time had already begun (Acts 2.17, where 'in the last days' is Luke's rewriting of Joel's prophecy).

e. Vielhauer did not discuss the problem of Luke's understanding of the Spirit in contrast to Paul's (see Chapter 4). Luke does not reflect the depth of Paul's understanding of the moral effects of the Spirit, but, as I have argued, he was presenting the missionary message of Paul rather than his teaching for converts.

The case that Luke has misrepresented Paul's theology is unsuccessful. What the discussion shows is that Luke has expressed only certain areas of Paul's preaching and teaching, and that he was not a slavish follower of Paul right to the point of using his terminology. Luke was his own man, doubtless not a profound theologian like Paul, but certainly not misrepresenting him in any serious way.

To say all this is not to deny that there are continuing problems in Luke's depiction of the history and theology of the early church and of Paul. At the same time, it does suggest quite strongly that Luke's intention in writing was not to promulgate a personal theological position that involved serious misrepresentation of the early church and Paul. Hengel is right when he sums up:

> The radical 'redaction-critical' approach so popular today, which sees Luke above all as a freely inventive theologian, mistakes his real purpose, namely that as a Christian 'historian' he sets out to report the events of the past that provided the foundation for the faith and its extension. He does not set out primarily to present his own 'theology' (*Acts and the History*, pp. 66-67).

Luke and his Sources

In the light of this discussion we can return to the question raised briefly in Chapter 1 and left unanswered: who wrote Acts? Since the major obstacles to authorship by someone associated with Paul have been shown to be far from impregnable, the way is open to suggest that the early tradition which names Luke the physician as the author of the Gospel and Acts is more than a piece of mistaken second-century conjecture.

The question of the authorship of Acts is closely tied up with that of sources. At the one end of the spectrum of opinions we have the view of scholars like E. Haenchen, that the author of Acts had little, if anything, in the way of written sources and did the best he could with a rather thin set of oral traditions. On this view, the passages which are written in the form of a first-person plural narrative are generally regarded as employing a literary device to convey the impression of eyewitness testimony by somebody who was not actually present. At the other end, we have the possibility that the author had contact with the early churches and some of the actors in the story. Those taking this view would hold that the 'we-passages' reflect first-hand information, whether from the author himself or an informant.

For myself, I find the arguments for this latter possibility the more convincing. If this view is correct, the author of Acts was in a good position to write about the early church and has done so as a genuine historian, that is to say, as an author who has given us his interpretation of what happened rather than a simple chronicle of facts.

Whether or not this conclusion is accepted, there seems little doubt that the question of the historical basis underlying Acts, which was prematurely closed by an earlier generation of scholars, is once more a legitimate subject for investigation and cannot be ignored.

Further Reading

F.F. Bruce, 'The Acts of the Apostles: Historical Record or Theological Reconstruction?', *ANRW*, II.25.3 (1985), pp. 2570-2603.

H.J. Cadbury, 'The Speeches in Acts', in F.J. Foakes-Jackson and K. Lake, *The Beginnings of Christianity* (5 vols.; London: Macmillan, 1920–33), V, pp. 402-27.

M. Dibelius, *Studies in the Acts of the Apostles* (London: SCM Press, 1956).

H. Harris, *The Tübingen School* (Oxford: Oxford University Press, 1975).

M. Hengel, *Acts and the History of Earliest Christianity* (London: SCM Press, 1979).

C.J. Hemer, *The book of Acts in the Setting of Hellenistic History* (ed. C.H. Gempf; Tübingen: Mohr, 1989).

G. Lohfink, *The Conversion of St Paul* (Chicago: Franciscan Press, 1976).

R.N. Longenecker, *Galatians* (WBC, 41; Dallas: Word Books, 1990)

G. Lüdemann, *Paul, Apostle to the Gentiles: Studies in Chronology* (London: SCM Press, 1984).

—*Early Christianity according to the Traditions in Acts: A Commentary* (London: SCM Press, 1989).

I.H. Marshall, 'Luke's View of Paul', *Southwestern Journal of Theology* 33 (1990), pp. 41-51.

W.M. Ramsay, *The Bearing of Recent Discovery on the Trustworthiness of the New Testament* (London: Hodder & Stoughton, 1915).

S.G. Wilson, *Luke and the Pastoral Epistles* (London: SPCK, 1979).

6

THE HERMENEUTICAL
PROBLEM OF ACTS

IN THIS INTRODUCTION to the book of Acts we have tried to understand it as an ancient text for a group of readers different from ourselves, and our approach has been affected by the kind of scholarly ways of understanding texts that are currently in vogue; had this book been written thirty years ago, for example, some of the matters discussed in the first chapter would not have been raised at all. The prime concern has been to understand Acts on the level of its final composition, but this has meant looking at it in relation to the history which it purports to record, both in order to gain an understanding of these events and also to understand the author's composition better in the light of what he has done with the materials on which he was working. But now we must briefly ask about how we understand what the book of Acts may have to say to us today. Are there any principles for answering such a question? And is it even a legitimate question?

Today it is increasingly recognized that no study of an ancient text is altogether free from the influence of the student's situation and pre-conceptions; each one of us has a perspective from which we view a text, and this dictates the angle from which we see it, the methods of study that we use, the things that we see and the things that remain outside our vision. Part of the task of interpretation is therefore to come to terms with our perspective and, so far as is possible, to recognize the existence of other perspectives and to understand them. Granted that the exercise can never be wholly successful, since even in looking at other people's perspectives we cannot completely abandon our own, dialogue between students with different perspectives can help to lead to conclusions about the text which are reasonably objective.

At the same time, it is perfectly legitimate for us to ask about the significance of a text from our own particular perspective and thus to approach it in a way which leads to fresh understanding of the text. Equally, we may find the text putting questions to us in our situation. Here in fact is where the text itself may alter our perspective and open us up to fresh insights. So there is nothing unscholarly or prejudiced about, say, twentieth-century Christians in Scotland asking what the book of Acts has to say to them today. Indeed, to fail to ask this question is to fail to engage fully with the text and to leave part of the task of interpretation undone.

The book of Acts raises this question in a particular way for us in that, more than other books in the NT, it is a combination of description of the early church and of teaching by early Christians. Paul's address to the church leaders at Miletus (Acts 20.18-35) is didactic. Many Christians would assume that what was said then can be reapplied to church leaders today, and would ask how these words are to be appropriated by them in their different situation. It is assumed that there is sufficient in common between the two audiences to make reapplication a viable option. But the account of the church at Antioch (Acts 11.19-30) is a description of a situation rather than a piece of teaching, and the same Christians might ask how far the description of a situation is intended to be understood as a paradigm to be followed.

This question has particularly arisen in connection with the charismatic movement, from which voices have argued that the patterns of conversion and Spirit-reception accompanied by such signs as speaking in tongues are meant to be normative for the church today. Other interpreters have equally insisted that the church should be primarily guided by the explicit teaching and commands in the NT rather than by sporadic examples. J.R.W. Stott (*Message of Acts*, p. 12), for example, says that we must look for teaching on the relevant issues, both in the immediate context and elsewhere in Scripture. On this view the problem is not significantly different from dealing with teaching passages which themselves must be understood in the light of other teaching.

Stott is, to be sure, an interpreter who believes that the NT in all its various parts does contain authoritative teaching for the church today. A different set of questions arises where the interpreter queries the value of some parts of the NT or finds them to be in intolerable tension or even contradiction with other parts. Thus it has been argued that the picture of Paul presented in Acts is so different from that given in Paul's letters—so contradictory in fact—that we are compelled to choose between the domesticated, tame Lukan Paul and the original, dynamic Paul.

The obvious first step in dealing with such a claim is to ask whether the alleged contradictions really exist. Even if there are differences in presentation between Acts and the Pauline Epistles, it does not follow that we cannot learn from both bodies of material (I.H. Marshall, 'An Evangelical Approach').

A greater problem arises with passages like Acts 5. This chapter causes considerable difficulties for many modern readers because it presents phenomena that they find not only bizarre, but also morally and spiritually perplexing. Here we find a picture of Peter in which he has the authority to voice the Lord's judgment against Ananias and Sapphira for their lying to God, and forthwith the judgment is effected, apparently without opportunity for repentance (contrast Mt. 18.15-17). Later in the same chapter sick people are carried into the street and placed where Peter's shadow may fall on them so that they might be healed (cf. Acts 19.11-12 of Paul). Peter is presented as a kind of superhuman figure with supernatural powers. Such people are not found as church leaders today (although some TV evangelists may have claimed to do similar things), and the kind of conduct which Peter practises or allows would not be acceptable to most Christians today; no church leader today is going to say that God has struck down a recalcitrant sinner or encourage sick people to sit in his shadow. The question also arises as to whether these things really happened, or have been correctly reported (did Ananias and Sapphira have sudden heart-attacks which the church interpreted after the event as a divine judgment on them?). So what are we doing when we make such comments on this section of Acts?

It is essential that such passages be seen in their first-century context. It can be noted that the description of the discipline would not have seemed so surprising in the first-century context, when equally tough discipline was administered in (for example) the Qumran sect. It can also be urged that the intention of the passage is to stress the enormity of the sin, and that the question of repentance and the like does not lie within the horizon of the story. It is certainly possible in the ancient world that a church leader might have been regarded as endowed with such supernatural powers that he could have acted in this way. Elsewhere Peter is credited with the authority and power to raise the dead. Stott argues that the action of the people who put the sick in the way of Peter may have been somewhat superstitious, but he refuses to regard it as a belief in magic; rather they had faith to recognize that the power of God was working through him. Gooding argues that it was essential to warn people that a blatant sin against the Holy Spirit was serious, but that such a judgment was quite exceptional in order to vindicate the presence and power of the Spirit in the church.

Other commentators urge that the kind of discipline practised here is not compatible with the procedures laid down for the disciples of Jesus elsewhere in the NT and that the summary act of judgment fails to have the kind of positive disciplinary character that is recommended elsewhere; even in the case of the man who is 'delivered to Satan' in 1 Corinthians 5 the aim is 'that his spirit may be saved'. Thus the problems in our passage arise not necessarily because some modern moral standard is being applied, but because in the light of the rest of the NT the difficulties stand out. This means that the Christian will not turn only to Acts 5 in dealing with the problem of sin in the congregation but will bear other passages in mind also. Acts must be read as part of the canon and not taken simply on its own.

At the same time, we are still left with a passage which ascribes summary judgment to the action of God. Do we say that Luke was wrong so to understand the character and activity of God, and that God did not act in this way? Or do we say that this passage challenges any soft understanding of God which divests him of a judgmental role? Or, again, should we say that God worked in that kind of way in the first century to convey the seriousness of sin to the church, because in that context this was the only way in which they could be brought to understand it, and that in our world he acts differently?

Whatever our answer to these questions, we need to be aware of the danger of feeling at liberty to relativize the teaching of any part of Acts if we have a mind to do so, simply by looking for other NT teaching which can tone down its impact for us. Where the teaching of Acts stands in harmony with the central teaching of the NT, then there is all the more reason to take it seriously.

Thus, it is surely the case that the emphasis of Acts on the need for the church to engage in mission 'to the ends of the earth' is something that needs to be recovered today. Equally, the emphasis in Luke–Acts on the rich tackling the problems of poverty in a radical fashion, which P.J. Esler (*Community and Gospel*, pp. 164-200) has so powerfully brought to our attention, must be taken up in a church which claims to be based on the teaching and example of the New Testament.

Further Reading

P.J. Esler, *Community and Gospel in Luke–Acts* (Cambridge: Cambridge University Press, 1987).

I.H. Marshall, 'An Evangelical Approach to "Theological Criticism"', *Themelios* 13 (1988), pp. 79-85.

INDEXES

INDEX OF BIBLICAL REFERENCES

Psalms			*Acts*			4.24-31	77
2.7	57		1.1–6.7	27		4.30	58
16	58		1.1–5.42	29		4.31	48, 69
68.18	66		1.1–2.47	29		4.32	78
110	56		1.2	43		4.34-36	78
110.1	56		1.8	29, 43		5	103, 104
			1.14	77		5.1-11	78
Isaiah			1.24-25	77		5.4	78, 81
53	57		2	26		5.31	57, 60, 61
53.7-8	57		2.4	67		5.32	67
			2.17	97		5.36-37	88
Matthew			2.22-36	56		6.1–11.18	29
18.15-17	103		2.22	60		6.1–9.31	29
			2.23	59		6.1–8.1a	29
Luke			2.25-32	58		6	34, 69, 87
1.1-4	38		2.33	66		6.1-6	78
1.1	32		2.34	56		6.3	67
1.2	66		2.36	60, 61		6.5	67
1.35	60		2.38	58, 67, 68		6.6	77
2.11	61		2.40	59		6.8–9.31	27
3.1	22		2.42	26, 77		7	69
7.13	61		2.44-45	78		7.56	65
12.11-12	79		2.46-47	77		7.59	61
13.34	75		3.1–5.42	29		8	26
19.41-44	75		3.6	58		8.4-25	70
21.12-15	80		3.13	57, 60		8.4	26, 65
22.19-20	57		3.15	57, 61		8.14-19	67, 68
22.28-30	93		3.16	57		8.14	26
22.33	26		3.17	59		8.18	67
24.34	61		3.19	59		8.25	70
			3.20-21	58		8.26-40	70
John			3.22-23	56		8.29	67
4.22	40		3.26	57, 59		8.32-33	57
			4.8	67		9	91-93
			4.12	59		9.15	70, 92

INDEX OF AUTHORS